Earth, Water, Fire, Wind

Our Connection to Mother Earth

Earth, Water, Fire, Wind

Our Connection to Mother Earth

Little Grandmother

(Kiesha Crowther)

eaRth
cDoΣheR
PUBLISHING

Published by
Earth Mother Publishing
7 Avenida Vista Grande B7
Santa Fe, NM 87508

Edited by Hans and Irene Brockhuis

Web: www.earthmotherpublishing.com

This book is dedicated to the great loves of my life, my wife Joyce and my two children Hannah and Jordan Crowther who, with considerable patience and support, allow me to do the work I do.

To the Indigenous Elders from around the world who spend their lives dedicated to the ancient ways and traditions that we all so desperately need to understand in order to heal what is wounded. I love, honor and respect you.

To the Great Mother Herself, I am grateful for all that you have endlessly given, all the lessons you taught me and the constant life and love you provide to us all. I dedicate my life to you, with all my heart, respect and devotion.

Contents

Introduction

Since the dawning of humanity our ancient ancestors held the answers regarding how to live in harmony with our planet and knew the true understanding of what it meant to be a human being. We once understood the most precious and important connections that unified us with our planet and each other.

Long before man made religions and the concept that belonging to that religion would make you more worthy or acceptable in the eyes of God, there existed one central belief. A united and absolute understanding that this Earth, this Sacred Planet is the Mother to all of us and without Her, we could not exist in a human form.

It is my profound believe that in order for us to heal ourselves and the damage we have created to our beloved Mother Earth, we must first learn how to love and respect her once again. We must learn from the old traditions in order to go forward. We must look back to our ancient ancestors and what they once knew and held precious in order to heal the deep wounds we each carry within ourselves today.

That ancient wisdom still exists today within our indigenous cultures who continue to teach and practice living in harmony with nature, wildlife, the elements and the four directions.

How many of us find ourselves living unfulfilled lives, searching for answers in a sea of social media telling us that if you only had this product or that "thing" you will find happiness? We were all raised as small children having been fed ideals that made us judgmental of others and of ourselves.

We have been taught to judge ourselves and place value on the way we look, how we dress, how much money we have, how many things we own and what our job title is worth by society. We have lost our way and our connection to what is real and what is really important. It has happened to all of us in one form or another. From the moment we entered the school system we quickly learned what box we would be expected to fit into. We were instantly put into categories. Ask yourself, were you the dumb kid or the smart kid, the popular or unpopular, the weird or acceptable kid? We grew up believing what someone else taught us to believe about ourselves. We were not taught that each of our gifts are unique and different and equally worthy. We were not taught that we are beautiful, because of our differences, but rather we must all fit into one box, that of society.

Albert Einstein said: *"Everybody is a genius, but if you judge a fish by its ability to climb a tree, it will live its whole life believing that it is stupid."*

This is a perfect example of how our educational system has failed us. We are not all the same and we should not be made to conform into being the same. This one belief alone has created a great chasm in our human society so massive that we have forgotten our own potentials, our own worth as individuals and our own greatness as a beautiful creation of Great Spirit and Mother Earth.

So how do we fix it? How do we once again get into the place of knowing our true selves and our connection to this planet and each other? How can we find our own self-worth and joy in living this life? The answer is much easier to find than one might believe. The truth is we have been taught to look for the answers in the wrong places. You will not find the answers to these questions by studying a course or passing a test that will give you a grade or title that others can admire you for. The answers will come by letting go of the ego and what society tells you is important, by letting go of what others think of you and finding your own connection to your own heart and soul. You will find the answers you are looking for by searching in the one place you never thought to look, but has been surrounding you your entire life... Mother Earth!

A very powerful way to begin your path back to Mother Earth and our ancient knowledge is by learning from the indigenous people and those who have been taught the old ways of respecting and honoring Mother, Nature and the Elements. One of the most profound ways in which we can honor Mother Earth and ourselves is by simply taking the time each day to face the four directions and give thanks for that direction, its coinciding element, color and meaning. It is such a powerful and necessary practice. Many indigenous or tribal people will not start their day without reverently offering their prayers and connecting to the elements and the four directions. Each tribe, clan or group of native people offer their prayers in slightly different ways and manners, but the overall meaning and understanding are the same.

For nine years now, I have been traveling around the world, learning and listening from different indigenous cultures and peoples. I have constantly been humbled by their almost unfathomable wealth of knowledge and understanding. Too many of us "westerners" think of the indigenous traditions as a second rate or nonfunctional way of creating change; in fact, they use the most powerful tools and practices to reconnect and begin the healing process with deep meaning and dedication. I remember the humbling experience of performing a Despacho Ceremony with the Incan Shaman

Don Alejandro from Peru. Performing a Despacho Ceremony is a way to communicate directly with the elements of nature by giving gifts and prayers to Pachamama, 'Mother Earth'. On white paper, we offered beautiful gifts such as flowers, seeds, herbs, cotton, corn, and sweets, all arranged into the shape of a mandala, made with great care and infused with many prayers for Mother Earth. When all offerings were in place they were bundled up in beautiful cloth and tied with string and offered to the Sacred Fire. All those who participated stood with their backs to the fire while Don Alejandro said the prayers, and the bundle was burned away and received by Mother Earth.

Another poignant moment for me was spending time with the Kogi Mamos, the great Earth Keepers and Elders from the Sierra Nevada de Santa Marta, situated deep in the Columbian Jungle. I was taught the importance and necessity of offering gifts to Mother Earth. Sitting in reverence with a small piece of their Sacred Cotton on my knee, I was shown the significance of envisioning what I would like to give to the Mother. (The complete opposite of asking for things which most of us do while praying). We sat quietly offering large quantities of pollen to pollinate flowers, minerals to enrich the earth, seeds to be spread across the grasslands, gold (which they believe carries the memories of Mother Earth) and crystals to help empower the energy grid, many healthy species of fish in the oceans and thick, stable ice around the poles to balance the temperature of our planet. With each prayer, we held our hands to our hearts, then stretched out our arms and opened our palms to allow those prayers to flow from our fingertips into the Mother as if water was pouring from a stream.

Kogi Roberto and Mariana (their Spanish names)

explained how the Kogi dedicate most of their waking hours in deep meditation, connecting to the Sacred Mother and offering her endless gifts. They stressed how important these practices are because not only are you envisioning and creating a healthy happy planet with your intentions, but you are also making a real and emotional connection with the living Mother. The Mamos are amazing people! They sleep for only three hours a night and eat very little food dedicating their whole lives to understanding the great Pachamama. In my opinion, the Kogi have always been and will always be the most profoundly dedicated and connected people to the natural world that has ever existed. Their knowledge about our planet, the flora and fauna and even our solar system baffles the greatest scientists from around the world.

Another great lesson came while spending time with a small group of Aboriginal people in Australia. One early morning as we walked slowly through the forest one of the women named Auntie Lila suddenly grabbed my arm and gestured towards an outcrop of large boulders in a wide-open space. I wasn't sure what I was looking for as I scanned the rocks. Soon she said: "You hear that? You see that?" I looked and listened the best I could, then looked back at her with questioning eyes. She just gave me a crooked little smile and nudged her chin forward for me to look and listen again. I strained a bit harder and to my surprise, I did hear something! It was a distant 'click' sound, then another. It was a very distinct sound used in Aboriginal 'corroboree' or ceremonies and made by what they call a 'bilma' or clapstick. I thought my mind was playing tricks on me, so I listened again and sure enough the sound rang out time and again. Something or someone in those rocks was playing the clapsticks, but I could not see anyone! I looked at Auntie Lila, and she said:

"You hear it, yea?" I smiled and nodded my head. Then she told me: "Those are the ancestors playing!" I looked back again to see if I could see who she saw playing, but I saw no one. She shook my arm and gave a light playful laugh and said: "No, no man be there; the rocks are playing for us." In the short time we spent together she instilled in me such a reverence for all living things. She taught me how to recognize that all things (even the rocks) are sacred, important and very much alive and interacting with us. The Aboriginal people have an amazing connection to the land. They do not believe that they own the land, but the land owns them and that all things share the same soul and spirit.

After having spent time with the indigenous Truku and Atayal peoples in the high Taiwanese Jungles, I gained deep respect for their ability to live as one with nature. When first arriving in the jungle of the Truku and Atayal people, I couldn't help but notice the colorful birds coming and going from the communal area and the monkeys clambering down out of the jungle canopy totally unafraid of us, the new visitors. This magical place was alive and in total harmony. Such a contrast to the bustling cities we had just left behind us. The small wooden buildings were built in such harmony with the forest that they seemed to almost melt into their surroundings. The young people from the tribe gathered together and shared with us their ancient songs and dances. Their arms and legs weaving and interlocking representing the interconnectedness of all forms of life on earth. Once the dancing and singing were over we slowly made our way down the narrow path to our little hut nestled alongside the thick jungle edge. No sooner had I laid my head down on the pillow than I heard a deep crack followed by an earth shaking rumble. Huge rocks fell from the cliff high on the mountain. We laid still listening to the sound of large trees snapping like twigs as the giant stones made their way down to the small valley where we were located. We could hear the larger stones hit the base of the valley with one last great thump. The smaller stones however, continued to trickle their way through the thick vegetation until coming to a stop at the back of our hut. The next morning after being greeted by the Chief of the tribe we asked about the rock slide the night before. He simply smiled and explained to us that the mountain itself was sacred and very much alive. There was no panic, just a simple knowing that the mountain had a rhythm and movement from time to time as it saw fit. The immense co-existence between the Truku and Atayal people and the animals, the forest, water and their beloved mountain was a testament to their "Oneness" with Mother Earth. Such a contrast to our "entitled" way of thinking in which we must control everything and bend it to our will. The Truku and Atayal people do not try to control their Sacred Mountains. They do not climb to the top of the mountain and proclaim that they have "concurred" it! They respect and honor the mountain as a sacred, living being that they share their lives with.

I could name countless experiences in which I have learned great lessons and examples from indigenous peoples from around the world. The most amazing to me is that there is a unified theme that runs through all of them. They are not consumed with what happens in the afterlife or with the dogma of a certain religion. They do not spend their lives obsessed with thoughts on what their past life might have been, what life might exist on other planets or what the latest fashion craze is. They do not devote their lives to what society might think of them. Instead they care for, respect and love the Great Mother and learn from the natural world. We can all contemplate the great mysteries of where we came from and where we will go after this life but let us not be blind to the life we are actually living and the Earth that is so graciously supporting the life we have. The wisdom of our indigenous peoples teaches one simple truth. We are all connected in the great circle of life, and this magnificent and Sacred Planet is Mother to us all. If we want to continue as a species, we must take care of, learn from and love the natural world.

No matter where I go on this beautiful planet and no matter what tribe or Indigenous Elder I learn from, the one constant teaching is that of honoring the earth, the four directions and elements. This knowledge is essential for our own understanding about the coexistence and interconnection of life on earth and where we the human being fit inside that wondrous circle of life. Elders from all over the world have begun teaching the importance of remembering who we are, how we are connected and how to bring back that which is sacred in our lives. Many of these Elders are the first of their tribe to teach outsiders, their "little brothers and sisters" as the Kogi would say. They are walking out of their jungles, their forests and coming down from their mountain tops to teach us how to respect the natural world again and how to bring healing back to our planet. They are pleading with us to return to our Sacred Sites, to perform the ceremonies and offer the prayers as our ancestors once did. They are asking us to pray not only for the healing of Mother Earth but also for our own hearts to reconnect to the sacred rhythm of life. They know how critical and time sensitive it is to take action now, if we are to stand a chance of rebalancing the health of the natural world in which we all depend on.

It is not every day that the world's leading Indigenous

Elders send out a worldwide plea for us to return to our Sacred Sites. So when they do we must listen! Many people have asked: "What if I cannot find a Sacred Site near me?" The answer is simple: "Make One!" No matter where you live, no matter who you are, no matter what your age or background is, you all have access to Mother Earth.

Within these pages, I hope to reignite a deep and resounding sense of connection to the Sacred, to Mother Earth in all Her wondrous splendors and to your own beautiful and purposeful self. You are much greater than you know, you are a literal spark of the Devine, a child of this earth and a brother and sister to all life that resides here. My hope is to reawaken the sleeping wisdom that lives within you so that you remember you are not separate from Mother Earth, but a very real part of Her. The elements that create, move, shape and change our planet also live within you! You have a purpose. You have a passion, and you have the ability to create the world you want to live in.

The Structure of This Book

Part I, "The Four Directions, Elements and You," offers a deep understanding of how each of the four elements plays an essential role for the health and purpose of our planet. We will learn how interdependent they are to one another and how each element represents itself in the human being. With the knowledge of who we are, what gifts we have within us and how we are connected to this Sacred Planet of ours and the elements that sustain Her; we can better understand how to communicate with the natural world. One of the most powerful ways in which we can do this is through creating our own Sacred Site or Medicine Wheel. You will learn the meaning of each element and at the end of each chapter you will learn how this element is represented in your own personal Sacred Site or Medicine Wheel. You will learn how to construct your own Sacred Site where you can offer your prayers and connect your heart, body, mind and spirit to Mother Earth.

Part II, "Ancient Sacred Crystals around the World," focusses on the importance of crystals and the ceremonies I have conducted around the world. I was given several Sacred Crystals when becoming Little Grandmother to place in specific, high vibrating locations to connect ceremonies and prayers into the planetary energy grid. In this section of the book, I will be sharing the detailed stories of where these crystals have been placed and what purpose they serve in helping the healing of humanity and our beloved Mother Earth.

Part III, "What Can We Do?", shares detailed information and in-depth research of what we each can do to create a healthier and more sustainable planet to live on. By making small changes to our lives, we can greatly impact the health and healing of our world. For many of us, we believe the world's problems are much too big for any one of us to change, but in fact, simple and small changes to our everyday lives can make an enormous impact for all!

Part I

The Four Directions, Elements and You

The Element Earth

The Element Earth is the first and most important element for each and every one of us to understand, because it is the Earth that provides and contains all the other elements. We often think that the elements are external from ourselves, but this is not true. We may have forgotten the old truths, our ancient wisdom, but it has not been lost. It is time to rekindle that fire of knowledge inside of ourselves and to walk in our own knowing of who we are and what it means to be a human being.

When we think of the element Earth, we think of the soil, the trees, and the plants. We think of our planet. Do we ever stop to think the element Earth is also a part of us? The element of Earth represents our human body. We ARE Mother Earth. It is time for us all to remember that we are not, we have never been nor will we ever be separate from Her while we are human beings. When we learn to love Her, we learn to love ourselves and each other. When we really understand She is the one giving us our human existence, we begin to respect each other, protect and love one another and this beautiful planet we all call home.

Our ancient ancestors remembered these truths, and their vast wisdom is still being held sacred and taught by our indigenous people. They know that their bodies do not exist without the Great Mother. She is still honored in many ceremonies, prayers and dances by our indigenous people around the world. She is respected above all other living things, because she is the source of life. How often do we stop to think that we, just like our ancestors and indigenous peoples, have the same Mother? It is time to reconnect the lifeline between ourselves and Mother Earth. In order to do this, we must understand who She is, and that we truly are Her children. We must learn how to rekindle our relationship with Her. When we come to know Her once again, we will love Her and with loving Her; we will honor, respect and protect Her. She is identified by many names: Mother Earth, Pachamama, Kishar, Tlazolteotl, Gaia, Coatlicue and Humahuaca. No matter what corner of the earth you travel to, you will always find a sacred name for the Earth Mother. She is the oldest deity known to mankind. Our ancestors knew Her well; they knew how to live with the Sacred Mother in a harmonious way. They understood how to connect with Her and how to have a true and very real relationship with Her. Mother Earth was known as the sacred feminine and the Mother of all creatures great and small.

Our species once had a great knowledge of who She is and of our place in the circle of life. We understood the four elements and their precious teachings. Throughout time, we as a whole have put aside or completely neglected, the old ways and the most essential sacred teachings of the indigenous tribes and wisdom keepers. We have even neglected our own hearts. We have traded the sacred for worldly things and concepts, for money and praise, for prestige and meaningless status. Most of us fall under this category not because it was our conscious decision but simply because it's the way we were taught.

It has taken many years for the human race to cut away the umbilical cord between Mother Earth and Self. Sadly, we are living at a time where religion and society have all left Her behind and as a result of that, the masses are blinded by untruths. Many of us haven't even stopped to realize that we lost that innocent connection to Mother Earth from childhood while growing up. As children, we all talked to trees, the insects, to animals and sang and danced when we felt joy. Now we are simply wandering this planet with hollow hearts, and we don't know how to fulfill ourselves. Although most of us were raised to think and act in a way which was suitable for our community, culture or religion, we now have the responsibility to become aware of the damage we are doing and to make a significant change.

This is why the Elders have called our generation: "The Strongest of the Strong." It takes great courage to stand up for what is right, to stand for something in the midst of the chaos society continues to feed. We have damaged our planet to a dangerous tipping point, to a place where She cannot sustain our selfish way of living any longer. We place more value on what society thinks of us regarding fashion, body image, job title and religion, then living a happy, connected and balanced life. We as a whole rate our self-worth by the things that we own and the status we can obtain, yet those are the very things that are damaging humanity and our planet the most.

The question I have asked myself my entire life is: "How can we do this?" How can human beings neglect and blindly create such monumental damage to the very planet that is giving us life? The answer to this is simple. We tend to neglect the things we do not love. We cannot love something if we are not aware that it even exists! How many of us are aware that Mother Earth is a living breathing being, a life source to each and every one of us?

We are the great consumers on this planet. We consume everything around us in extreme quantities. Society teaches us that the more you have, the more you are worth. We are taught to fill the void of happiness inside our hearts by feeling the rush of spending money, buying that new pair of shoes or that one more accessory. Simply put, we have been brought up to believe that "things" can make us happy. We are constantly thinking that: "if I only had ____, then I would be content." At the end of the day; consuming will never fill us up! The raw truth is that you cannot love yourself until you know yourself, and you know where true happiness comes from. If you do not love yourself, how can you truly love anything or anyone else? If you do not love something, why or how would you care for it, protect and honor it?

Throughout the years of traveling around the world, I have become aware of another very painful realization; one that cannot be dismissed or kept silent. The neglect of the feminine on our planet, in our religions and in our cultures is disturbing to say the least. I have found, the places on our beautiful Mother Earth that have been heavy polluted, abused and neglected are also the very places the feminine has been treated in much the same way. You simply cannot visit a place where the streets are covered in garbage and the rivers reduced to floating sewers without noticing that the women throughout the area are treated just as badly. One of the many examples of this that I have personally witnessed was in Egypt.

Egypt and the Feminine

As a child I was hopelessly addicted to watching the wildlife TV series "Wild Kingdom" and David Attenborough's "Zoo Quest." I would often imagine myself right there with him in the tall grass of some far-off country or floating along the Nile in a dugout canoe. Watching these programs and reading the National Geographic magazine (I would save up for every month with my allowance) was my favorite thing in the world. I was always fascinated with Egypt in particular; of the Nile in all its grand splendor, the Great Pyramids, date palms and beautiful sand dunes. Sadly, shortly after arriving in Cairo my childlike view of Egypt had swiftly faded away.

Upon arriving in any new country the first thing I do is step outside and locate a tree or a little secluded patch of earth to offer my prayers and to connect my energy to that of the earth in that location. Stepping outside the doors of the Cairo airport however was a shock to the system. I immediately began looking for that special spot in which I could start my prayers only to find there were no trees at all, nor was there a single patch of soil without garbage. I reluctantly bent down and began clearing a small spot of earth from its trash and cigarette butts so that I could begin my prayer when I noticed things were about to get a lot worse. Seconds into saying my prayer the whistling and taunts began from the men who were now making their way towards me. One man even had his hand inside his gallibaya (long shirt worn by Egyptian men) touching himself.

I quickly stopped what I was doing and stood up looking for the entrance to the airport about thirty yards away. A wall of men was blocking my way towards the entrance, and I wasn't about to walk towards them. My eyes started searching for help when I spotted my savior. He was a little, peaceful looking grandfather with a short cut white beard sitting against the wall with a cane in one hand and another hand reaching out for me to come. I knew instantly he was genuine and gentle. His eyes were filled with love and compassion. I took his hand and he slowly walked me to the entrance of the airport paying no attention to the men who continued to laugh and make kissing sounds towards me.

I knew then and there that I wasn't in Kansas anymore! That is when our dear, sweet travel guide Mohammad and his brother Abdul gathered our little group and let us know that we should not go out alone, and we should always stick together. We loaded ourselves onto the bus and began our travels through the city of Cairo where the shock of the situation became even more apparent. I was truly struck, almost speechless at the amount of garbage and filth that covered every inch of the earth. It was as if my mind couldn't comprehend what I was seeing. This was not what I saw as a child in my books and on TV. This was no longer my dream but my nightmare. At no point on our drive to the hotel could we see the earth beneath the amount of garbage on the sides of the road or walkways.

The horses used to pull the carts were so thin they couldn't stay standing. Dogs and cats were emaciated. Instead of earth lining the great Nile and tributaries, only mounds of trash could be seen for miles. At one point, we saw a tractor at the edge of the tributary digging into the river bed and pulling up buckets full of black slime infused with garbage being hauled to the edge to create the river bank. It was so heart wrenching I had to pull the curtain. I sat there in the bus literally shaking from the reality that surrounded me when someone yelled out: "There are the pyramids!" We flung open the curtains and looked up into the sky where we could see the top of the pyramids! They were so big and so astounding; my mind could not comprehend the size of them. We all stared out of the window not saying anything just in awe of what was in front of us.

Amidst the constant honking and sudden braking in the traffic and all of our excitement, we hadn't noticed that we made it to the Luxor hotel. It was beautiful! We stepped out of the bus and onto a sprawling green lawn when the smell hit us like a wall! The punishing and powerful smell of exhaust and pollution in the air was so overwhelming that even our eyes started to burn and water. It was like standing directly behind the exhaust of a city bus and taking a deep breath.

Later, we were told that breathing one day in Cairo is the equivalent to smoking two packs of cigarettes a day. By the time Joyce and I got into our room, our minds and hearts were simply on overload, and we broke down and cried. It was just too much. The amount of garbage in the water and on the land, the smothering pollution, the total lack of love and care for the feminine and the animals was heartbreaking. Although we had been on a long journey across the city, we had not seen one other woman, not ONE! The respect for the feminine was lost completely. Egypt, the once proud and the most honored place throughout the world, was now a place of filth and disrespect for the feminine and Mother Earth. For me, I was already exhausted and the trip had not even begun.

At that moment, I didn't yet understand that this was just the beginning of what was to come. I loved being at the temples and Pyramids though, saying the prayers and performing the ceremonies. These moments were some of the highlights of my life. We saw ancient symbols of the flower of life set in stone in the Temple of Osiris at Abydos. To this day, it is not known how these symbols were set in the stone so perfectly. We witnessed hieroglyphs of flying saucers, helicopters and army tanks in the Temple of Seti at Abydos. We met the old caretakers of the pyramids and temples, and we were allowed to go to many secret and sacred places.

This was a trip of contrasts. We had many amazing experiences and life-changing moments alternated with moments of disgust and disbelief. Out of all the important work we were able to accomplish, and things that we were blessed to see in Egypt; my heart still aches from the total neglect and disrespect to the feminine. During the entire trip, I only saw three little girls; one had her arm cut intentionally so she could ask for money; another girl (not more than 3 years old) was dressed in a beautiful pink dress and was told by her father to dance for us while he asked for money; the third girl was being chased outside a tourist shop by the shop owner holding a board embedded with nails.

On two separate occasions, we had men who worked at the hotel entering our room unannounced, standing at the end of the bed and looking at us. Another pushed the door open to look at Joyce while she was changing her clothes, and I had to physically push him out of the door and into the hallway. The scariest moment was on the Nile cruise. I had gone outside before heading to bed to say my prayers as I do every night. While standing at the edge of the boat giving thanks for the day a man grabbed me by my arm. He tried pulling me down the stairs. I luckily broke free and was able to run towards a Latvian couple on the other side of the deck. When reporting these incidents, we were told that some women who come from western countries and visit Egypt, are looking for sex with exotic Egyptian men, therefore, it was our fault.

This trip was very trying, on one hand, there were such great highs but also such great lows. I have never been to a country that lacks respect for women in such magnitude. Even while stuck in traffic on the bus the men outside would touch themselves while looking in at us through the bus window. We had to leave a temple site, because unknown armed men had been following our tour bus to that temple. On another occasion one of the members of our group was told that his passport would be taken away and destroyed, and he would be left to die in the temple, if he didn't stop arguing about the existence of human beings being on our planet less than 6000 years. We were also told that the hieroglyphs of tanks, helicopters and UFO's was a "mistake caused by erosion." It was all very much the best of the best and the worst of the worst.

I do not want to give the impression that I believe all people in Egypt are bad. This is not true. Our guide Mohammad, his brother Abdul and his mother were some of the nicest and most loving people I have ever met in my life. It was just a great and unmistakable lesson in the phenomenon that, when a culture does not respect the feminine, they do not respect Mother Earth and vice versa. Never have I seen the earth treated so poorly, nor have I ever seen women treated with such cruelty. These two things go hand in hand. Anywhere you go on the planet and you witness the earth being treated with neglect, I can guarantee that the feminine will be treated in the same way. I watched as people ate their bag of chips or meal out of take away boxes then just drop the garbage on the ground and continue with their conversations. This was total and undeniable disregard for the planet. For me, it was a shock to the system. I had never seen such disrespect for the natural world. The saddest part about it is that these are not the only people; this is not the only city or the only country that has such disregard for the environment. How many times have you seen someone throw garbage out of their car window? I simply do not understand how anyone could do something like that. Nature is not a trash can! There are only two explanations for this kind of behavior in my mind. One; being total and complete ignorance of what you are doing and how your actions affect the world (a child who copies the actions of his or her parents). Two; being selfishness, the absolute lack of compassion, respect and care for the animals, plants, soil and water, that your garbage will have an undoubtable effect on because you were too lazy to place it into a trash can.

We have forgotten to respect and protect our Mother Earth because we have forgotten She is a living, loving source of our life. She IS our Mother! When we sit down to a beautiful meal and we eat, do we stop to thank Mother Earth for the meat, vegetables, fruits and grains that she has provided for our bodies to sustain our lives? When we take a drink of water does it cross our minds that this is a pure gift from Mother Earth to give our body energy and life? Every meal you have ever eaten, every drink of water you have ever swallowed and every breath of air that has filled your lungs has been a pure and selfless gift from Mother Earth. Water is not man made; oxygen is not man made; our food is not man made! No human being can live without these things yet very few people are trying to protect the very thing giving them these vital necessities for life. For the majority of the population, it is a concept that has never crossed their minds. They treat the planet as if these resources are infinite, not something that has to be protected and sustained.

Take a moment to think about the woman who gave birth to you, your physical mother. Feel how much you love her, considering all she has done for you, the life she has given you, the help and constant care she has provided from the day you were born until this day. Would you at any moment degrade her? Would you throw trash at her? Would you take more from her than she could possibly give? Would you abuse her or let others abuse her? The resounding answer is always "NO." We would never think of doing something so atrocious to our own mother. We could never let anyone else do something so terrible to the woman who has loved us so profoundly. Then, how is it that we allow ourselves and others to degrade, abuse and dishonor the Great Mother who provides for us all?

We all have forgotten to honor and respect our Mother Earth from time to time, even us, who consider ourselves spiritual or connected. Most of us simply forget throughout our day because we are consumed with our everyday tasks, what needs to be done, our jobs and the constant buzz around us. I am not saying that we should lose our focus on our daily lives and tasks, but we should become more aware of the brilliant life that is around us while being in the midst of those tasks. Every living thing in nature has a place, serves a purpose and is relying on and giving to the circle of life. We must learn how to see through the hustle and bustle and take time to notice what we are being freely given day by day by the Mother. When we learn to love the Mother and appreciate all She is giving, we learn to take care of her.

Circle of Life

The great circle of life in all its complexities is truly incredible. Every species of flora and fauna genuinely depend and rely on each other. They are without a doubt, interdependent on one another, from the largest tree to the smallest fungi. Out of the millions of species on our planet, there is not one without great importance and purpose. Each and every one plays an integral part in the eco system. In many ways, human beings forget this great chain of life and how it relies on each player to create a whole. Take, for example, the plight of the Brazilian nut tree. It is illegal to cut these trees down in three countries. They are left standing alone in a vast sea of uprooted, barren deforested soil. The governments pat themselves on the back and say: *"We saved the Brazilian nut tree,"* having no clue or simply turning a blind eye to what they have really done.

You see, there is only one species of animal that can break through the seedpod of the Brazilian nut once it has fallen to the forest floor. That is a very special animal called the agouti, no bigger than a house cat. It specializes in the ability to chew through the extremely hard and extremely thick seed pod where it can get to the very nutritious nuts. Once the agouti has gotten to the nut, it will eat one out of 20 and bury the others where these seeds will germinate and grow into a new Brazilian nut tree. That is not all to this miraculous story. Before a seedpod can even grow, the Brazilian nut tree must be pollinated. This can only be done by another wonderful interconnected relationship; between the Brazilian nut tree, the orchid flower and the male orchid bee. The male orchid bee is attracted to the orchids that grow on the upper tree branches in the canopy. The male bee is drawn to the smell that the orchid gives off, knowing that female bees will only mate with the male who smells most of the orchid flower. Only the male orchid bees can pollinate the orchids. The females, on the other hand, pollinate a completely different species, the Brazilian nut tree! Once a year a large white flower appears on the nut tree attracting the female bees who are one of the few insects which are able to open the flower to get to its pollen. The interconnectedness is amazing! The Brazilian nut tree needs the agouti down below on the forest floor to open and disperse the seeds. The agouti needs the female orchid bee at the top of the canopy to open and pollinate the Brazilian nut tree's flowers in order to produce a seedpod. The female orchid bee needs the male orchid bee which in turn needs the orchid flowers! This is one example of so many countless and complex relationships in our diverse ecosystems. We simply cannot leave the one tree we like standing and log all the others thinking we are saving the species. That's simple ignorance. Without the intact forest, there is no agouti, there is no bee and no orchid flower to sustain life for the Brazilian nut tree. We need to be aware of the great importance and purpose of each and every species in order to create a healthy and diverse planet. We cannot save a species from going extinct if we cannot save the eco system in which it lives. What good does it do to try and save the orangutan if we cannot stop the cutting and burning of their jungle forest by the palm oil industries? How can we expect to save the mountain gorilla while we continue to clear cut the last bit of forest it has to live in? We must begin protecting entire eco systems in order to save these animals because each species, flora and fauna rely on each other to survive and thrive.

This is also true for humanity, as we are all interdependent on one another. There is not one human being who is menial or lesser than another. We all depend on each other, in all of our diversity and complex relationships to create a healthy and intact humanity. As human beings, we tend to value ourselves on what we perceive as greatness, but do we stop and take the time to see that even the smallest of gifts are great? Every connection, every relationship, every lesson and gift we give and receive in this world is vital and important. The largest tree in the forest does not evaluate and classify the other species and their role in the forest as greater or lesser than the other, but interacts and rely on the whole to work together to survive and multiply. Nature is selfless; it is pure in form and is a total and absolute generous provider. There are no hierarchies nor subservient categories. Nature works with and supports all species. In truth, there is no death of anything, just a beautiful circle of life!

How many of us remember the movie "Avatar"? I can't tell you how many times I heard people saying how amazing it would be to live in a place like that. A place where all the trees and animals were connected and could speak with the people and where the plants glowed with fluorescent colors. The truth is, with the exception of being in a giant blue body, we do live on a planet that amazing! Our trees, our soil, our plant life and our wildlife are all connected with the ever flowing abundance of Mother Earth's energy! Everything on this planet is connected to this massive circle of life; the incredible web and stream of micro fungi in the soil; the nitrogen given to plants and grasslands from waste products from animals; the amazing process of photosynthesis and the life-giving oxygen that trees and oceans create; countless numbers of shark, eels, shrimp, algae, corals, fish, fungi and insects glowing with bioluminescence. We do live in that magical world; we have just stopped seeing it! We are not simply haphazard life forms that crawled out of the ocean, and by some miracle of chance have been given this planet and all of her resources to use and consume at will.

We need to wake up! We are amazing, conscious and miraculous beings. We are divine sparks of the Great everything. We are cosmic beings, who get the opportunity to be here with this Sacred Goddess Mother Earth. We get to experience being Her child for just a moment in our eternal journeys as the Great I AM. We are not separate from Her but are part of Her and the great rhythm of life. We human beings have been given great gifts; the gift of speech; the gift of arms to hold and legs that can carry us from one experience to the other; consciousness, free will and choice. However, we are not the greatest species created. We are not free to take and destroy what ever we wish. Anyone can clearly see the effect we have on this planet as species that are irreverent and out of balance with our surroundings. We have ripped ourselves out of the Great Circle of Life.

We do have great gifts, but with great gifts comes great responsibility! By being human we have been given not only free will and choice but the greatest gift of all, the ability to act. How we choose to act is up to every single one of us in the short amount of time we are here. We human beings are a species with the ability to act consciously and with this gift and responsibility, we can cause an incredible amount of damage or of healing. The human being is the sole creation living on Mother Earth who creates garbage, acts irresponsibly, takes more than is needed, abuses and neglects. We are the only species on the planet that acts out of ego. What we forget is that it is a choice; it is a choice to use these great gifts for positive or for negative. As the human race, we have a responsibility to be the caretakers of our Mother Earth and all Her creatures, great and small.

When we can truly understand who we are as children of the one Great Mother, many things start to become clear for us, and we can start shifting our awareness as well as our actions and become a healthy member of the circle of life. We need each other just as the Brazilian nut tree needs the agouti, and the orchid flower needs the bees. With our words and deeds, we are influencing each other and shaping each other's lives. When we start to value and love ourselves and each other for our differences and with our individual gifts, we become a healthy part of the circle of life.

The beautiful Mother Earth is a very special place with great diversity, interconnected relationships, ecosystems and elements. She is the Mother to us all and our greatest teacher.

The element "Earth" is not only my favorite but also the container of all other elements, so to understand the others we must begin first with EARTH.

The Element of Earth

The element of Earth is for each and every one of us represented in our human bodies. We must understand and fully comprehend that we are not separate from Mother Earth; we are Mother Earth! We are Her children, and we exist as human beings in these beautiful bodies because She is sustaining them, supplying them with Her energy and is giving us life, every single day. So in order to respect and love Mother we must first know She is alive, and secondly we must love and respect ourselves. For most of us, it is easier to honor and love Mother Earth, to see Her as perfect in all Her aspects of love, beauty, compassion and even Her storms. Do we truly love ourselves in the same regard? Do you truly feel that you, all of you, is perfect? Can you love yourself for all that you are, for what you perceive as good or bad throughout all the experiences you have had in your life?

So many of us do not or cannot love ourselves for who we are. We do not take the time to realize that everything we have been through, good or bad, has made us who we are today. Instead, we think of all the mistakes we have made, the things we wish we hadn't done and all of the reasons why we are sinful, bad or unworthy. The truth is very simply—there are no mistakes, only learning and growing opportunities.

I want you to take just a moment and think to yourself how many times throughout your day do you believe or say something negative about yourself? From the time you get up in the morning and look in the mirror until the time that you fall asleep. How much of your energy, your thoughts and emotions were negative or positive? In a lot of cases, we focus way too much of our energy on the things we believe we have done wrong or what we want to change about ourselves instead of accepting ourselves for who we are and the lessons we are learning. There is a huge difference between focusing on a goal and trying to better our lives through our spiritual and educational growth and beating ourselves up for what we do not know or do not have. We are much too occupied with worrying about our work, our status, our looks and our things that we forget to value ourselves for the brilliant beings that we really are. Religion has taught us that we are sinful, and we deserve punishment if we make mistakes or do something that is not in accordance with that religion. But can you imagine how much your life would change if you stopped beating yourself up for the "mistakes" you have made and started loving yourself for the journey of learning and growth you are on?

We are here to be human beings, not to be perfect or to be in a constant state of enlightenment. We are here to learn and grow, to fall down and get back up, to break our hearts, to fall in love and to even fail from time to time. It's all about learning, about growing and bettering ourselves. We should enjoy being a human being. We should enjoy this journey and enjoy being who we are. We should love our bodies in all their shapes and sizes and learn to love ourselves for the Divine beings we are. Life is undeniably not easy. We have to learn as we go, and as we get older, the lessons get harder, just like in school. If we were to stay in kindergarten year after year, how much would we learn? Not a great deal—so we continue on and each year it is a challenge and the tests get harder and harder, and sometimes we fail at the test, and sometimes we pass.

The challenges in life will never go away. We will constantly be given lessons to learn. How many of us, throughout our lives, have found ourselves asking: "Why does this keep happening to me?" Well, it's because your Great I Am is giving you a lesson to learn—a learning and growing opportunity. If you do not learn the lesson the first time, it will come again and again and again until you do. You see, everything in life, every event, every moment of every day, is given to you by the one thing that loves you the most and the one thing that knows you better than anyone or anything ever could: YOU! Your eternal spark of the great everything, your highest self, your soul and spirit, your Great I am and eternal connection to Great Spirit knows exactly what you need and when you need it. It is YOU giving yourself every moment of every day and every lesson. So if your Great I Am sees fit to give you a lesson, you will be given that lesson to learn as many times as you need until you have passed.

There is no God up in heaven that looks like an old man with a long white beard, dressed in a white robe who says: "You must go to earth. It is going to be very, very hard. You must live a perfect life, or you don't get to come home. Oh, and by the way, there is no such thing as a perfect human being except for Jesus Christ, so good luck." NO! This certainly did not happen. You chose to come to this planet. You chose! You chose to come here and experience what it would be like to live on this planet, to experience duality, to experience the good, the bad, the hard and the easy and to learn and grow. You came to have relationships, fall in love, and break your heart. You chose to come here to express your passions. You had a purpose and a plan as to why you came. So do not think about the challenges or lessons in your life as punishment. Do not think when something is hard it must be "karma from a past life, and you must pay the price." Be present to this life, dear friend, this life is what matters. You are here now in this body, taking these lessons in the here and now, so be present to the now. I can say with absolution that no one knows for sure what their past lives were or what choices were made during that life or what form you even took during that life. Blaming or claiming a past life to build your ego or excuse the present challenges will get you nowhere. What is important is to be completely awake to this grand test you are taking called "life on planet earth." Be present in every moment, every challenge be it easy or hard; you are here to learn, and you are the one who chose to come.

There is that old saying: "You cannot see the forest through the trees" and for most of us, this is true. We get so wrapped up with the everyday nonsense that we do not stop to see ourselves from a higher perspective. If you can just stop for a moment and view your life from a higher place, you can then start to see where you should give your attentions, your energy and emotions to. From this place, you can see that you are perfect because of all you have lived through, all of it— not just what religion or society has taught you is "good or bad." Literally take a moment to lie down somewhere quiet and undisturbed. Imagine yourself, your Great I Am looking down from the place we call heaven and be a witness to the life you have had so far. See yourself as a small child, where you lived, what life was like, the lessons you went through. Then see yourself as a teenager. What was life like for you? How were you learning and growing? What were the events in your life that shaped you? Now as an adult, observe your life, the decisions you have made, the challenges you have gone through. Who you have become. Take a moment to truly be a witness to all you have learned and grown from.

Looking at your life from a bigger or higher perspective helps you to see the meaning of your challenges. It helps to see what has made you strong and how it has created you to be who you are today. When you stop beating yourself up over the past or the mistakes you seem to have made and stop wishing you were someone else—only then you can truly love yourself. In truth, there is no such thing as a mistake. Everything you have been through has made you who you are. Own it! Be proud of yourself and the things that you wish to change or the things that are lacking. Don't beat yourself up for those things that make you feel sinful. Because you are not sinful. You are learning and growing like everyone else who has ever come to this planet. When you can let go of the self-judgment and giving all your energy away to the things you wish were different and start owning who you are, you will see how perfect you really are and how all of your experiences in the past have led you to become who you are today.

One of our biggest faults in life is that we are always comparing ourselves to other people. We think, if we were only as wise as that person or only as spiritual as that individual. If only I had the things others have, then I would be happy or deserving. We put people on pedestals because of what they have achieved in life instead of focusing on what WE are achieving in life. No life is the same; no journey is the same; no challenge is the same and no matter who you put on that pedestal; I can guarantee you they have their own lessons to learn. In truth, no one is free from lessons and hardships. That very thing is what makes us all perfect! Your life is perfect; your journey is perfect. We are all learning day by day.

Instead of being upset that life is so hard, simply

understand that you are going through a lesson to learn and grow and to better yourself on this journey. As I said, life is hard—this is true for all of us. There is no lesson, no level of life that is better or less than the other. You can be in first grade in your lessons of life, just beginning to learn your alphabet, or you can be graduating from college and getting your master's degree. Is one better than the other? Is the child worth less love and respect than the graduate? Of course not! Is the student worth less than the teacher? No! We each are learning at different levels, and we are equals. So instead of focusing our attention on other people and their growth, we need to focus on ourselves no matter where we are in our journey of learning.

Too often we spend our lives comparing ourselves or rating ourselves to other people, for better or for worse. No matter what lessons you are learning and no matter what grade level you are at in life, it is as it should be. Society has taught us whom we are allowed to judge harshly and whose actions are acceptable or not acceptable. For instance, what do we automatically think of the drunk on the street asking for money? Is it different from or harsher than what we would think about the millionaires who turn a blind eye and walk past the man in need of help? Often we are so fast to place judgment on people and their challenges, but in truth, no matter what it "looks like" are we not all being tested on some level? Why do we think the lesson of overcoming addiction is worse than the lesson of learning compassion or how to share abundance? Each is a lesson; each is a challenge. The person suffering from addiction must learn a very hard lesson about dealing with pain, suffering, loving their body and valuing themselves, not to mention it being visible to everyone. Versus the man or woman who has a great amount of material wealth in life with the test or challenge of being generous or greedy, the ability to help or hinder many lives. Material wealth does not make one person better or less than the other, but we do tend to devalue the person who is suffering from poverty more than a wealthy person. This is a sad fact that society has taught us to believe in.

We have all been taught that those living in high society or polite society are above and beyond the status of the norm. For instance, when you think of the alcoholic with an addiction problem, what image comes to mind? For most of us, it's the poor middle-aged man in an old t-shirt, unkempt and unclean with a beer in his hand, right? This is what we automatically think of an alcoholic, but in reality, the Centers for Disease Control (CDC) and the National Center for Health Statistics (NCHS) show us that the rich out drink the poor by a staggering 24.7%.

What do we automatically think about the wealthy person whose challenge in life was to help or hinder others? I know for myself, I like to think that the wealthier you are the greater good you can do, but sadly the Bureau of Labor Statistics data shows us that the poorest households contributed an average of 4.3% of their incomes to charitable organizations, and the richest gave less than half that rate, 2.1%. There are so many examples of how we have been trained to think— the more money you have, the more things you have and the more popular and beautiful you are—the more worthy you are of acceptance.

The truth is, none of us really know what someone else is going through in their lives, what challenges they are facing. So we have no right to judge them. We have to throw away our judgments and look at each other as brothers and sisters and beyond that; we must look at ourselves and our own challenges and respect them. No matter what you are going through in life, no matter what the challenges are, know that your soul is learning and growing and that all is as it should be. You should never feel less than someone else because of what you're going through but honor yourself and the journey you are on. Take the time to understand what the lesson is about and what you can learn from the experience. Don't put yourself down because of your trials, or blame someone else for the challenge we find ourselves in.

It has almost become an automatic reaction to simply place blame on someone else for the situations or "the lessons" we find ourselves in. No matter what the situation, no matter how hard or how ugly, only you can be responsible for how you act and react. We tend to think that by blaming someone for whatever situation we find ourselves in, we no longer have to be responsible for our actions—this is never true. We are responsible for our actions, reactions, feelings, words and personal growth on this planet. Placing blame or anger on someone else whether they caused the circumstance or not, doesn't change or fix the life lesson you are taking.

I remember being in South Africa with the Chief of the Khoisan people when he made such a clear point on this subject. Sitting there with his calm and wise demeanor, beautiful bald head and round belly, he looked at me and said: "If a man sits in his hut with his wives and children with no food to eat but one potato, should the man be angry at the world for not giving him food? Should he expect a neighbor to work for food and then give it to them while they wait in the hut? Should he expect a stranger to show up and save them? Should he be angry and yell and complain about not having food and that no one is solving the problem for him? Should he expect food to fall out of the sky because he prayed for food? Or should he plant the one potato so that it can grow into many potatoes and feed his family?"

We all know the answer to these questions, don't we? How many times in our lives do we sit and complain about our situation or our problems yet do not take responsibility for them or even pray for something and expect to just receive it without putting in any work? We can always look at the problem or situation we are in and begin to learn and grow from it, not just blame someone else or expect someone else to change it for us. We must change our anger and blame into "what can I do to learn from this and how can I change the situation?" We can sit at home and complain about the world, or we can be the change! We cannot go to the grocery store and buy a cheaper cut of beef that comes from the huge cattle industries then sit at home and complain about the mass cattle industry causing deforestation, high emissions and pollutants! We cannot say we are against child labor while wearing a t-shirt manufactured by the children forced to make it. We cannot be outraged that our bees are dying because of pesticides and then swat one the moment it gets too close to us or buy the fruit that has been sprayed with deadly pesticides. We have to be the change if we want to see a change. We have to be responsible for our actions in all situations. We have to plant the potato!

No matter who you are, no matter where you live, no matter your circumstance, if you can remember that your trials and your lessons make you who you are, and only you are responsible for the outcome you can start learning, growing and loving yourself and your life. When you can truly love yourself for all that you are, you can start to truly love others for who they are, what they are going through and honor them for their own journey without judgment. When we can let go of judgment on ourselves and others, we open the door to the capability of immense love and acceptance for all, and we can find ourselves as united beings—unified with not only our brothers and sisters but also with our Mother Earth.

Just as we must learn to understand what life really means and how to love ourselves and each other on all our many different journeys, we also need to understand and love the Great Mother. Most people would say these are two separate things, but in fact, they are one and the same. Mother Earth is providing you with this body, with your food and water, with the air in your lungs, with your human experience and all other living creatures great and small. So in learning how to love yourself, you start loving Mother Earth. You simply cannot love yourself without loving Her and you cannot love Mother Earth without loving yourself. Your Body is Mother Earth. You are the Earth Element. So the biggest question for us all is: do we really know our Mother?

Do we understand that every plant and animal great or small is alive, has a soul and a spirit, a purpose and a function? I think for all of us, if we see something is growing or green; we know that it is alive—do we know it also has a spirit? When we begin to understand that all things are alive, all things have a spirit and a purpose, we start to appreciate and protect those things more than we did before. There is a practice that I feel is so very important for us all. A practice that helps us to stay connected and will remind ourselves throughout our busy lives that there is a world much bigger and much more significant than what we tend to see and focus on. It is much more important to FEEL this practice rather than just reading it as a concept—so I ask that instead of just reading this and moving on in the book, you take a few moments to go outside and really feel your way through the practice after reading it.

Your Sense of Self

Find a comfortable spot outside and sit or lie down on beautiful Mother Earth and close your eyes. Once you have slowed your breathing and cleared your mind of the outside world and all the chaos, I want you to find the sense of Self within. Feel who it is you are and where your sense of Self is. With your eyes closed and feeling your sense of Self I want you to imagine for just a moment that you were born to this wondrous world without legs.... Now ask yourself: "Am I still here? Do I still exist? Is the sense of Self still there?" Feel where YOU are inside your body; is the sense of Self still there inside of you even though you have no legs? Of course it is! Now imagine you were born without arms as well.... Are you still there? Imagine that you were born to this body without having a mouth to speak, or eyes to see. Let your face become a blank slate. Is the sense of Self still there? Do you still exist? Of course you do; your sense of self does not exist in an appendage and is not related to the size or shape of your body, the color of your eyes or hair. It exists within.

Too often we believe that who we are is what we look like, our outward appearance, our beauty, our clothes, our money, our image and our things. We have been taught to believe in ourselves with what someone else told us to believe. In truth, it has nothing to do with who you are! You, the real you, your sense of Self, your Great I AM; your soul and spirit live inside you and that sense of Self has existed forever and will continue to exist forever in many different shapes and sizes and lives. Our bodies are a great gift from Mother Earth and without Her; we could not have these bodies. We are human beings living in a physical form of flesh and blood while we are here on earth, but YOU exist on a much bigger level and came from that brilliant source of the ALL, God, Great Spirit, Oneness, whatever you wish to call it. Each and every one of us have chosen to send a spark of ourselves to this world to experience this test, to live and learn from this journey. All of us!

As you sit there with your eyes closed, feel your sense of Self again…. Who it is you are, the spark of your own Great I AM, your spirit and soul. Imagine that great place you came from, the source of all light and love, all life and oneness. Feel what it is to be a part of the ALL as a pure form of infinite light and creation. Be in that moment for a little while and feel your great sense of self; then when you are ready, imagine making the conscious decision to send a small spark of yourself from that light of oneness to the beautiful Mother Earth, just as you did before so many years ago to gain this body you are now living in. Allow yourself, while you drift closer and closer to this beautiful planet covered in wondrous blue oceans, green alpine forests, sandy deserts, tropical rain forests and rolling grasslands, to slowly and softly land.

Imagine in your conscious mind, that this time your sense of self awakens inside a tree. You have arrived and are ready to learn and grow and experience life on planet earth. Feel what it is like to be inside that tree, feel your branches stretching out and your leaves soaking in the light. Your roots growing deeply into the soil taking in the moisture and connecting with the nutrients. As a tree, you have countless relationships and partnerships. Feel what it is like to provide life to all the life around you, giving sustenance to the insects, the birds, the fungi and shelter for so many others. You are alive and are a great intricate part of the circle of life on Mother Earth. As a tree you do not have legs to walk or eyes to open and see, you do not have a mouth to speak or arms to grab and hold, but you are alive, you exist, your sense of self is STILL THERE! Just as you did when you imagined your body without legs or arms. Who you are, the essence of self is not your body; it lives within your body and that same sense of self, that spark of a living soul, lives within every creature and every plant great and small.

Slowly come back into your body and sense of Self in the here and now, feel your legs and wiggle your toes, feel your arms and hands, open your eyes and look around. Look at all the life that surrounds you, from the smallest blades of grass to the biggest tree. Everything around you that is alive has a spirit, a spark of life. Although they cannot speak with words and cannot walk or embrace you, they are still here! They still exist!

It is true; nature has never stopped speaking to us; we have simply stopped listening. No matter where you go on this beautiful planet, all life, all of nature is constantly speaking to us. Not with human words but through emotion and feeling and through heart consciousness. This is why our indigenous peoples and Elders speak of listening to the forests and the waters. For centuries, prayers have been offered to nature and lessons learned from being quiet and gaining great wisdoms from the unseen. Nature can speak to us, it can teach us and give us insight into our lives and show us the way to any question we have. We simply have to be quiet and listen. Too often we think in our egotistical ways that only what we can see must be true. If we take the time to truly look and truly listen, a whole new world opens up to us. When we start to appreciate and really understand and see all the life that is around us, we learn to become the protectors and not the owners of our beautiful world.

Recently, I was in Hong Kong and China, giving several lectures and workshops. On the last day of giving talks, I was so exhausted, I found myself standing in a grove of giant cottonwood trees questioning if I could finish. I started to pray to the Great Mother to give me strength when I noticed a small piece of cotton from the cottonwood tree swirling above me, then dropped straight down in front of my feet. Such a small thing, this little seed wrapped in its cotton cocoon as it lay there at my feet. When I studied it, I began thinking about how amazing nature is. That this tiny speck of a seed could grow into the giants who stood all around me. I knelt down and tucked the seed into the damp soil knowing that if I could muster the energy to share the message for just a few more hours, who knew what that little seed of knowledge in someone, could grow into. So I stood back up, did the earth breathing meditation and headed back into the building.

It wasn't a profound, earth shattering, Blockbuster experience but simply nature speaking in her most pure and gentle way. Nature is constantly speaking to us, continuously teaching us and showing us the way. All of this knowledge is freely given. All we have to do is pay attention. The key to speaking with nature and listening for her teachings comes through a feeling. I cannot tell you how many times people have said to me: "I tried and tried to listen for the tree to speak, but I just didn't hear anything," or "Wow; I wish I could speak to animals like you but I never hear anything." I have to chuckle a bit and say you will be listening a long time if you're waiting for them to speak in words because it is not going to happen. As humans, we are so proud, aren't we? We think that in order for something to be real it has to be like us. Why in the world would a tree speak in English or Dutch or any other language? We are just a bit too arrogant sometimes. It is true; all of nature is speaking, just not with vocal cords. So how does it work? How can we all do it? Well, most likely you have already done it before but simply didn't know you were doing it. For example, how many of us have had a pet before? The animal couldn't speak to you, right? Not with words anyway. So how did you know when something was wrong with your beloved pet? How did you know if he or she was anxious, worried, sick, happy or at ease? You felt it! How many of us have children? Think of your child when they were very young, before they could use words. As parents we know inside when something is wrong. Our child could be in the next town or even in another country, and we KNOW when something is wrong; we know because we feel it, because we are so deeply connected to that child, because of the love we share. We are all connected with not only consciousness but with emotion. Each and every single person on this planet can re-teach themselves how to speak and listen to nature. It is a built-in gift that we all have had from the first person to walk the earth until today. We are forever connected to this planet and all life on it while we are in these human bodies. In order to speak and hear those other living things speak back to us, we must truly love those other living things.

I say, re-teach, because as children we knew how to do this. Think back to being a child and how easy it was to talk to our animals and to the trees. To sing little songs while we walked through the grass and have conversations with the flowers or the streams. We were all so innocent and open to the life around us, and then we grew up. We all got sucked into this vortex of trying to fit in, trying to go with the flow, trying to become what society expected of us and wanted us to be. So it was no longer acceptable to chit-chat with the plants and the animals, and we started focusing on what we were told was important.

Luckily, many of us have formed loving relationships with our pets that have kept this knowing alive inside of us. Do not fear that you have lost it or that this gift is gone forever. You just need to reboot it or simply flip the off switch back ON. We must first learn how to be quiet. Too many of us are so busy talking and thinking that we never find the calm that it takes to listen, truly listen and truly see. Until we can silence our minds from the white noise all around us and the thoughts of day to day issues, we will never be in a conscious place to truly hear with our hearts.

Walking in Nature

Being in Europe for a couple of years now I have witnessed an odd phenomenon. One that leaves me a bit baffled when it comes to people's concept of spending time in nature. It begins with the grand preparation, the "pre-walk ritual," I like to call it. The most important ritual of all is the mass consumption of tea or coffee followed by a dress rehearsal. One must wear walking pants, not just any walking pant but the ones that have a zipper at the knee in case one might find themselves in need of shorts while traversing the trail. Second, not any shoe will do. Only the best and most rugged of walking shoes made of water proof leather and insulated for Mount Everest conditions must be placed on the feet before strapping to the wrist a fashionable titanium walking stick. Then comes the fleece and rain jacket, fanny pack or back pack and finally with the last sip of tea the outdoorsman is ready to traverse the absolutely flat, heavily traveled and often paved path of the Dutch outdoors.

Everyone gathers at the edge of the path and is quietly proud of themselves for taking the time out of their busy schedules to go into the forest to be one with nature. Then off we go. That is when the oddity truly begins, we talk and we talk and we talk some more about our day and everything we have to do, our jobs and coworkers, our spouses and children. We talk about how great that coffee was and how good we are for being in nature. By the time the walk is over, and we make it back to where we started from, it is time for another round of tea and coffee while everyone talks about how great their walk was and how they "just love to be in nature."

How many of us can see ourselves in this? Even if you skip the "pre-walk ritual" and go do the walk alone—how many of us spend our time walking and thinking about everything we are worried about, everything that needs to be done, all of our life's duties and issues? Did you ever stop talking? Did we hear anything that nature had to tell us or learn anything from the life that surrounded you? Did you take the time to breathe in the energy that Mother was offering? Did you take the time to hear all the sounds nature was providing, all the life that was saying hello? Did you smell the earth, the green life bursting from the ground and the trees? Did you take the time to really see what was there and take a moment to send it love or receive love from it, or did you just talk? Taking a walk in nature and never being aware of it is like reading a book while singing along to the song on the radio. You will learn nothing from the book.

The point is we will never hear or learn anything if we cannot learn to be quiet. Being quiet in nature is of utmost importance because unless you still the mind and shut off random thoughts you will not be aware of the emotions and feelings that nature is speaking with. Once you tune into your own heart and the love and respect you have for the life around you, you can start seeing all the lessons surrounding you. You can start to feel the love that Mother and all of Her creatures have for you. You become part of the great circle of life and begin to understand that everything is one.

When we go for a walk in nature, it should be to clear our heads, to reconnect to the presence of Mother Earth. As you walk it is important to pay attention to all your senses, to awaken yourself to what it truly means to be a fully awake human being. Take time to stop and awaken all of your senses one by one. Pay attention to only what you can smell, then only what you can hear. Take a moment to feel your body. Feel the sun and the shadow on your skin, the breeze flowing through your hair. Feel the weight of your body on the earth. Finally open your eyes and witness all the life that surrounds you. Take a moment to take your shoes off and connect your feet to the earth and breathe in Mother Earth's energy. Hug a tree; sit for a moment in silence. Be grateful and feel love for all that surrounds you. Feel the love that the Earth has for you just as a mother loves her child. Take a moment to be that tree, that flower, that blade of grass; connect to Nature and to Mother Earth.

It is no accident that we are upright beings and that our feet are on the ground. Our feet are covered with thousands of the largest pores on the human body. Over 2000 on each foot. The entire body's structure can be accessed by different points on the foot. When our feet are placed on Mother Earth, the Mother energy comes up into the body, up through the chakra system and is shared to every part of our body. This is why it is so important to reconnect the soles of our bare feet to the earth. A lot of people forget that it is Mother Earth's energy that keeps your body alive and moving. We understand that our spirits, our souls that spark of the Great I am, live inside our human bodies. That spark is the true sense of Self. It is what connects us to all other life because its source is Source itself. Our physical bodies, on the other hand, are a gift from Mother Earth. We cannot have or sustain a human body without her food and water, as well as Her energy. Just like a hand inside a glove our spirits are inside our bodies, but without the energy running through us that hand inside of a glove would just lay there. Mother Earth's energy is what gives us the ability to move, talk, act and function. Many times throughout our lives we get low on energy. We get exhausted from the stress of our day to day life. We do not eat well. We do not sleep well. We do not connect to that life source energy that is all around us. We all wear rubber-soled shoes that do not allow Mother's energy to flow up from our feet into the body. Our ancient ancestors did not wear rubber soled shoes. They knew the necessity of staying grounded to Mother Earth's energy.

I am not saying we all need to go barefoot day in and day out. We do not live in a society that would allow that nor would it be feasible or comfortable to do so. However, we must remember to kick those shoes off whenever we can. Take a few minutes and do the earth breathing meditation that is so important to keeping our bodies healthy and strong. It takes only a few minutes a day out of our busy schedules to not only help us ground but also to keep our bodies healthy and strong and connected to the life-giving energy, that is always available.

Earth Breathing Meditation

We all need to be able to connect ourselves and regain our strength and balance throughout our lives. We often get ungrounded or low on energy and this is a perfect meditation to start each day. I often do this same practice before going on stage for a talk or before a ceremony to build up my own energy and ground as much as possible. I will also do this breathing meditation before prayer and honoring the four directions. It is a practice that can help us all to get our energy flowing correctly and helps to move blockages in the chakras and places where the flow of life energy has become slowed down or blocked. It also can help open you to spiritual guidance and prepare you for deeper states of prayer and meditation.

First, you need to stand with your bare feet on the ground, the soil or the grass outside. Start by breathing the color green, the color of Earth energy, up through the soles of your feet; feel this Earth energy filling your cells and nourishing every inch of you.

With your first in-breath, bring this green Mother Earth energy up as far up through the legs as you can. Then exhale it down and out through the soles of your feet back into the Earth. Do it as many times as needed so that you can really feel or imagine Mother Earth's energy starting to flow up into your body. On the exhale, let the energy flow back down out through the soles of your feet back into Mother Earth.

On the second breath, you will slowly breathe Mother Earth's energy up moving it even higher up to your first chakra or your pelvis area; then exhale it back down your feet and back to Mother Earth. When you breathe the energy in, really try and imagine or feel the energy coming up through your blood system, your muscles, your bones, surrounding your feet, your legs and up to the pelvic floor. When you can feel the warmth of the energy in your body you are ready for the next breathing step and that is to pull this energy up past the pelvis and bring it up to the lower abdomen, your second chakra. Breathe in and hold it there comfortably, then exhale back down your legs and out through your feet.

Bring, on the next breath, (your third chakra) the energy up to your high stomach, really try and feel it filling you up, then release it back downward into the Earth. Be sure to focus on each particular part of your body as you descend the energy; do not just skim over but visualize and feel the energy traveling down and filling your limbs, your muscles, blood, bones, and cells.

On the next breath in, (fourth chakra) bring the energy up to your heart and feel it circulating and penetrating your entire chest area, let it fill the heart completely before exhaling. Some of us need to do this more than once, and that is ok. Anytime you feel that the energy has not made itself fully present, simply breathe in again. When you feel relaxed and warmth fills you, then you know you can move on.

Breathe the energy of the next breath, up to your throat (fifth chakra) and let Mother Earth's energy flood open this area, which is connected to your voice and speaking your truth, spreading your passions and seeds. Then exhale it back down to the Earth through the bottoms of your feet.

On the next in-breath, breathe the energy up to the middle of your forehead between your eyes (sixth chakra—third eye). Feel this part of you, connected to spiritual vision, higher perception and intuition, opening and being gently caressed and connected to Mother Earth. Exhale back down into the Earth through the soles of your feet.

The final in-breath. Bring the energy all the way up to the top of your head (seventh chakra-crown) and feel the entire body filled with beautiful Mother Earth's energy. Be sure to fill your face, your eyes and ears, your brain, your pituitary, your hair and neck with this green nurturing light, connecting you to all of life.

On your final exhale, breathe the energy down your arms and out through your fingers and back into Mother Earth. This creates a complete circle of energy. This step is vitally important and should be done only at the last step once you have gone through all the chakras.

Now you are connected to the complete circle of life energy. This potent green life force energy can help you heal, revitalize, and balance your whole being. It is so important to do this step by step, taking your time at each chakra and do it as many times as needed. Feel the energy rising up before going on to the next step. Take your time to really feel the energy rise and fall with each breath. Notice, when you are at your final breathes, the warm and sometimes tingling feeling in your hands and fingertips as the energy flows from your crown chakra through your hands back to Mother. Now you are ready to start your day and take on any challenges that may come with a healthy and fully connected body.

Creating Your Sacred Circle or Medicine Wheel: Earth

We are going to begin with the element Earth, the direction West and its color black. The first thing you are going to do is finding a quiet, special spot for yourself outside. A place that is peaceful, where you can pray uninterrupted each day and where you can create a small Sacred Circle or "Medicine Wheel" for yourself. Remember, many native or indigenous people take part in the creation of their medicine wheel to honor and offer sacred prayers to the four directions. They all differ in small ways but no one way is the only way, there are no right or wrong means to offer your prayers as long as they are honest and pure. All prayers must be done from the heart and the soul of the person speaking the prayer. Each prayer should be personalized but one thing should always remain, and that is the reverence and the gratitude for all blessings that are given. There are many different ways a medicine wheel can be created, I will be teaching the way I was taught and the way that is closest to my heart.

I remember an Elder once telling me: "There is only one rule when it comes to performing a ceremony or offering your prayers and that is that you must do it perfectly. And the only way to do something perfectly is if it comes 100% from your own heart."

Remember, while creating your own Sacred Circle, you do not have to be with indigenous people. You do not have to perform a ceremony as they do. You do not have to use their words but rather pray and create from your own heart, offer your own deepest and most sincere prayers and you will be doing it perfectly!

We started this chapter with the element Earth, what it's meaning is and where this element lives within you. The element of Earth represents your physical body, the sacred carrier of your spirit and soul while on this journey as a human being. Once you have found the spot where you wish to offer your prayers and you have taken the time to do the breathing meditation, you will now slip off your shoes and place your feet on beloved Mother Earth and face the direction of the west. Feel, for a moment, your feet on the soil or in the grass. Be aware of the weight of your body. Take time to be grateful for the opportunity to experience being a human being. You are not just one out of the 7.3 billion living on this planet, who gets up and goes to work, eats and goes to bed. NO! Be grateful and aware that you are a true spark of the ALL; you are the Great I am! You are a wondrous spirit and spark of the Divine, a soul who came to Earth with destined intentions. A soul whose efforts and abilities can shift the consciousness of humankind. Whose love and gratitude can touch and heal the wounds of many. You are Great! You are unique! You are all that you can imagine! An unstoppable force of good and you have been given a human body, to live and breathe and experience the Divine Mother Earth and all Her amazing creatures.

In this moment, with your feet placed firmly on Mother Earth, you realize who you are and what a blessing it is to be here—to be able to witness and take part in all that you get to experience. Close your eyes for a moment and feel what it is like to have a body, to be on this planet. What it is like to be able to feel the warmth of the sun on your skin…, the cool breeze in your hair…, the soil between your toes…, just take a moment to feel and be grateful.

Now listen, shut off all other senses but what you can hear.

Many times throughout our day, we are too busy with life to even hear the creatures around us. Take a moment to pay attention and listen to all the life that surrounds you, from the rustling of the leaves, to the insects and birds calling out to each other, singing their song. Nature is always speaking; we simply have forgotten to listen. So take a moment and really listen to the conversations of beauty happening all around you. Now it is time to shut off all other senses but smell. Do you know what Mother Earth smells like? Have you ever thought about it? Do not be afraid, bend down and smell the earth, the rich dark soil, the green grass, the leaves and the trees. Smell the air. Smell the fragrance of life that is all around you. Taste the air, open your mouth and breathe in, taste the sweet air that fills your lungs. Place a blade of grass into your mouth, a small stone, a leaf. Take a moment to be grateful for the gift of taste. Now stand and slowly open your eyes and truly look at all the life that surrounds you! From the smallest insect to the largest tree, take it all in, look at all the splendor Mother Earth has created for you to enjoy. Too often we take it all for granted; we forget that our senses are one of the greatest gifts we have, and more often than not we only pay attention to what we can see. There is so much more! Stand for a moment and take in all the senses. Feel, listen, smell, taste and witness all that Mother is giving you and be grateful! To be in gratitude is the highest level of consciousness, it is the easiest and the most powerful way to ignite the feeling of love and high vibration of energy into the body. While you face the direction towards the west, take the time to be grateful to be a human being, have gratitude for your body and all the gifts that Mother has given you in this life.

Your body is the element of Earth. As a human being you

cannot, you have never been and never will be separate from Sacred Mother Earth. It is impossible. Yes, we can forget Her, but we can never be separated from Her…, because…, we are Her!

From the moment you were born into this body until the day that you pass away and your spirit returns to Source you will be a part of the Mother. She is not just some random rock orbiting a yellow sun, somewhere in space among the hundreds of billions of galaxies in the universe. She is a living, life giving and precious Mother to every human being who has ever been and will ever be. She is a planet of over 8.7 million different living species, species we are all connected to in the great circle of life. WE are so fortunate to share and experience this magical place for a bit of time in our soul's eternal journey.

Feel all the gratitude you can muster inside of yourself for this great planet—for the element of Earth and what it means to you, a human being having been given your precious body. The reason we face the west and associate this direction with the color of black is because this is the direction the sun goes down. It is the direction that brings us the time of night, of dreaming, of darkness and of meditation. The color black is actually not a color at all; it is the total lack of color that creates black.

The definition of black by Wikipedia describes it best: "In the visible spectrum, white reflects light and is a presence of all colors, but black absorbs light and is an absence of color. Black can be defined as the visual impression experienced when no visible light reaches the eye." Black, in most indigenous cultures, represents the beginning, emptiness, a time of meditation, shutting off the mind. From this place of emptiness all can begin, all can be given. So when we face the west, we are giving our thanks to the beginning of all creation, the creation of the Earth, the time of deep meditation and the purest form of receiving understanding from source. We are giving thanks for the creation of Mother Earth and for ourselves and our infinite connection to source by going back to the place of blackness, the place of meditation.

During my prayers, I always stand facing the direction I am giving gratitude for. Before I speak any words, I try my best to feel the deepest appreciation and the sacredness of the moment. Then and only then will I begin speaking the prayers out loud. I thank the direction of the west, all the ancestors, the wise men and women, the Elders, the grandmother and grandfathers, the spirits of the west for their ancient understanding and knowledge. I thank the element of the Earth and all She means to me in my life. I offer thanks for my body and the great and abundant gifts She constantly gives, the seen and the unseen. I thank the color of the West, the blackness from which all things are given.

After you have done this in your way, with your utmost respect, honor and in your own heartfelt words, you can offer your prayers and thanks in tobacco, either by smoking or by sprinkling it into the direction of the west. If something else suits you better, that is also fine. Just remember: something should always be gifted to the Mother and Great Spirit for hearing your prayers.

The most important thing is that these are *your* prayers, from *your* heart. Again, there is no set way in which you must pray, the worst thing you could do is speak some memorized prayer that comes from memory instead of from your own true heart. There are many examples of offering prayers to the four directions such as the Celts who also offer thanks to the tree spirits, the fairies or Fae folk. The Peruvian shamans also include the animal spirits of the four directions, the condor, the humming bird, the snake and the lama. Countless other tribes use different colors to represent the directions. The point is by doing this *from your heart* and you cannot go wrong.

When you are finished offering your prayers, you will need to find something to mark the area in which you stood for the west. A stone, a crystal, something natural that will represent the direction of the west and the color of black to begin your Medicine Wheel. As you place that first stone, kneel down to the earth and give once again your respect and honor and set your intentions for why you are creating the medicine wheel, this sacred place that you will come back to time and time again to reconnect with yourself and your Mother. Thank the West, the blessing of blackness and your Divine planet and remember how blessed, how important, how significant and how beautiful you are.

The Element Fire

When we think of the elements, we often simply think of wind, water, fire and earth but do we really take the time to comprehend what they truly are and how they influence our planet and each of us? We began by speaking about the Earth element because it is in truth the keeper of all the other elements, just as your body (Earth) is the keeper of the other three elements inside you. So, if the element Earth is our body—what is fire? First let us begin by thinking about what purpose fire has on our planet.

It is easy to think of fire as a massive ball of flames that shines down onto our planet to keep light and life continuing here on Earth. We also think of the molten, boiling mass of rock deep in the core of our planet. In fact, the element of Fire represents much, much more. I want to dive further into what this element truly is about, what it does and how it affects each of us as human beings. Again, what exists on planet earth also exists within us. Mother Earth and the Human Being cannot be separated. When we think about the element of Fire, we must ask ourselves what is its purpose? What does it do? What is its true power as a natural element on our planet?

Mother Earth is an extraordinary teacher. When we begin to rekindle our relationship with Her, we can begin to understand the boundless knowledge She is sharing. Take, for example, the enormous power of fire! Nature uses the fire from within to create flowing lava (on the surface of the earth) and magma (that which is under the ground) forming and constantly reshaping our Earth's surface. The element of Fire creates the most fertile soil on earth, recycles carbon dioxide (food for our plant life) and also creates hydrothermal vents that bring chemicals and heat from the interior of the earth to the surface, which in turn helps regulate the entire ocean chemistry.

When thinking of the Fire element we often think of the sun. We all know that nothing would be living on planet earth without the warmth, and the light that the sun gives us each and every day. However, have we ever thought of why we have and need wild fires? Most of us think that a wild fire is a bad thing, and we rush out with our fire trucks to put them out. Nature has a way of taking care of itself, and wildfires have been a part of Mother Earth's cleansing and renewing process from the beginning of time. Wild fires are extremely important to nature—to the forest and grasslands. These fires play a pivotal role in the circle of life. How many of us have seen a grassland or a field full of yellow, dead and dry grass in the spring, which has been set on fire either by man or nature? Our first reaction is: "Oh no!" Wait a couple of weeks, you will see that something amazing is happening. You will see that very same field or grassland has become greener than its surroundings. The old and the dead have been burnt away, its ash now being a fertilizer for the new plants, ready to grow green and strong again. The same goes for a wildfire in our forests. Without the wildfires, the dead debris of the forest cannot recycle itself fast enough and will eventually build up and choke the new life trying to grow.

For example, when you walk through a pine forest that has not had a wildfire in many, many years you will find very few new trees. The ground is choked with dead and fallen pine needles hindering the underbrush and smaller plants from growing and creating a healthy ecosystem; as a result, the forest eventually will start to die. In the natural world, Mother Earth will use the wildfires to renew herself. A lightning storm will strike and She will burn away the dead. This is a very important natural process for the health of an entire forest.

Another example of the importance of wildfires, is the story of the Jack Pine Trees (North American pine), which have resin filled cones that are very strong and durable. The cones remain dormant until a fire takes place and melts away the resin so that the cones can pop open and release their seeds. A couple of years after the wildfire, one can witness Aspen trees, new Jack Pine trees, fir and spruce sprouting up everywhere. Sadly, the Jack Pine trees and Aspen trees have been dying out in vast numbers because wildfires are now being controlled to a great extent in the northern hemispheres. Fire is an extremely important natural element for the health of our planet and also for us, the human being. Unfortunately, we have built homes and started entire communities in most of the world's forests, and Mother Earth's natural process has often been interrupted.

The discovery of making fire is without a doubt one of the most, if not the most pivotal moments in human history. With the use of fire came heat, meaning human beings could move into colder climates opening up new hunting territories. They were now able to protect themselves from the elements and from dangerous animals. It opened up living areas with the prospect and ability to eat new foods. The ability to use fire, believe it or not, literally changed our appearance into the way we look today. New foods and the ability to cook our meals gave us more nutrients. We lost the big barrel chest and wide set hips that we needed to support a large stomach and the heavy set of muscular jaws that were necessary to break down tough fibers. With fire came the capability to eat meat, which gave us protein and the nutrients to develop the growth of bigger brains. Early use of fire not only was used for protection, warmth and food but also utilized to gather together in communities under one hearth.

Our ancient ancestors as well as our indigenous cultures at present still gather around the central fire to eat, to tell stories and pass on important knowledge, rituals and the offering of prayers. Many of these ancient rituals can still be seen around the world—such as the burning of sage, Palo Santo, tobacco or other herbs and grasses for cleaning and clearing an area or person's energy. The Martu tribe of aboriginals in Australia still baptize their children in smoke rather than water. Every single one of us today have good memories of sharing a meal, cooking together or being in the kitchen with family. Fire is just as important for us today as it was for our ancestors. Behind every outlet, microwave, stove top, heater and automobile is a fossil-fuel burning somewhere. The use of fire at present is just as vitally important as it was for us hundreds of thousands of years ago. We can literally list hundreds of reasons why fire is such a powerful gift in our lives, but we can also list many reasons why fire can be a damaging and devastating force.

Fire can be one of the most destructive forces on the planet and can quickly get out of control if left to rage. It can become a violent devastation to so many, before it is stopped, or it burns itself out. Today it is estimated that less than 3% of wildfires are from natural causes, the other 97% are caused by human carelessness and negligence! Intentional arson, discarded cigarettes and unattended campfires are the top culprits of the wildfires harming our planet. When there are frequent wildfires in one particular area or region, the devastation on the ecosystem becomes apparent. Nowadays, forests are stripped of native plant species and consumed by other invasive plants that are more fire resistant. Forest fires create rising of carbon dioxide into the atmosphere to huge levels causing a more prominent greenhouse effect. Manmade wildfires deforest huge areas of land that become eroded. When it rains, this erosion causes flash floods, land- and mudslides and renders the top soil useless for new growth. In 2015, according to the National Interagency Fire Center, more than 8 million acres were burned in the U.S. through wildfires. Fire is a powerful element—it can be a creator, a cleanser and a regenerator, a giver of light and warmth, but it can also be a massive force of destruction when in disharmony with the natural balance.

Knowing what the element of Fire means for our planet, the question remains what the meaning and purpose of this element is within each of us? How is the element of Fire important and what role does it play in our lives? What does it represent for the human being? Our fire is our passion! Each and every one of us not only chose to come to this planet, to live this life, but we also came to this planet with passion and purpose. Every one of us has something inside that gives a sense of purpose—the things that we believe in and stand for. Those things that we love so much that the very thought of them makes our heart beat faster and gives us goose bumps. When I speak of the things that make you truly who you are, they have nothing to do with what you own, or your job title or what you look like or what others think of you. I am talking about who YOU are.

What makes your heart race? What do you stand for in this life? Why are you here and what do you LOVE? These are your passions in life. This is who you really are. Your passion in life is your fire, your flame and as long as your fire is ruled by your heart, your passions will give your life purpose and bring the world your gifts. When we think of the word "passion" we tend to automatically associate it with words like love, goodness and intimacy, but this is definitely not always the case. Are you not passionate when having an argument? Are you not passionate when trying to prove that what you feel and what you think is more important than another's thoughts or feelings? Are we not passionate when we are fighting or trying to convince others that our way of life is right and theirs is wrong? We can literally see passion in egotistical things as well. War, Religion, Money, Politics, the list goes on and on. These things and beliefs are all ruled by a passion that is instigated by Ego and not Love. Our Fire is the element that we must watch closely and constantly analyze while we live our lives. Just like a wildfire that can be destructive and out of control, so can our passion become directed by our egos. When our passion is ruled by ego, I can guarantee you that someone is going to get burned.

Think of the last time you were in an argument. Now ask yourself, why was I arguing? Were you in love, kindness, understanding and acceptance while in your argument? Were the words and the tone of your voice filled with compassion and care for the other person? How did you feel inside, was there joy and peace; or were you trying to prove that you were right and the other was wrong? Did you allow your passion to get so out of control, just like a wildfire becoming violent and devastating, bringing harm to yourself and others? Usually, when our passions are ruled by ego, our anger burns hotter and hotter until we say hurtful things that we would usually never say. In an argument, we want to not only prove that we are right but also that the other person was wrong.

In this case, the fire just gets bigger and bigger until no one can escape the burning flames, and the damage that it causes. Again, our fire can be the most brilliant light and warmth in our life; it can feed our souls by bringing nutrient to our hopes and dreams; or it can become the most damaging force to us and others.

One of the biggest examples of how our fire can hurt or heal us is by looking at our sexual history. There is nothing more damaging to an individual person or their family line, than sexual abuse. One out of three people today has been sexually abused. When a human beings sexual desire is ruled by ego, the flame will without a doubt cause some of the greatest pains known to mankind. Those who have been abused sexually know that nothing can be as damaging to our self-esteem, our self-worth. In many cases, sexual abuse causes extreme amounts of trauma to the body and the psyche, including great distress, anxiety, shock, fear, depression, moodiness and post-traumatic stress disorder; on the other hand, there is nothing more healing and beautiful than falling in love and making love. The sexual act within the genuineness of love can bring healing, not only to the heart and the emotions but also holistically, bringing the mind and body together, creating a calming security, a sense of peace.

Our fire ruled by love can bring forth the most exquisite pleasure and healing possible, and it is the most beautiful, most glorious, precious, intimate, wonderful act between two people that we will ever know. Used correctly our fire can burn away the old and clear and cleanse our past and make way for that new growth of life inside of us. Used under the power of ego, our fire will only create a consumption of all that is good and will simply burn ourselves and others. Our fires used with ego are not always as dramatic as the horror of sexual abuse, but often it raises its ugly head in our day to day lives in smaller ways.

Since childhood we have been taught that you need to "fight for what is yours," "never back down," "the strongest person always wins," "the loudest will be heard." We are taught to believe that we are not all equal and we should be judged based on our race, gender, sexual orientation, physical attributes, ethnicity and religious status. We were born into a world that places more value on the ego than on the heart. This is evident in our everyday lives—how we were raised in society. Although many of us are waking up at this time, there are still many people who think that they are socially superior to others, or superior due to their country, class, occupation, political party, social group, educational and wealth status or (the most ridiculous of all) their skin color. Having our societies teach us from a very young age to think and feel through the ego, we become like trained little soldiers living our lives this way. Luckily, there are many of us all over the world waking up from this illusion that has been keeping us blind to our own truths and potentials. We are finding ourselves at a great crossroad, a monumental jumping-off point as human beings; you can either follow societies, governments and religions into the abyss of destroying each other and our planet, or you can choose to take another path. That path is Love, love for yourself, for Mother Earth and all of our brothers and sisters.

Albert Einstein

When we are living in love consciousness, we once again start to believe in ourselves, the true meaning of who we are, how great we are and how we truly create the world we live in. To love genuinely is the most powerful energy in the universe! Can you imagine a world in which we all followed our hearts and truly understood the power of love? Albert Einstein, being one of the greatest minds ever to come to this earth, understood this more than anyone else. A letter written to his daughter Lieserl shows the true meaning of Love:

"When I proposed the theory of relativity, very few understood me and what I will reveal now to transmit to mankind will also collide with the misunderstanding and prejudice in the world.

I ask you to guard the letters as long as necessary, years, decades, until society is advanced enough to accept what I will explain below.

There is an extremely powerful force that, so far, science has not found a formal explanation to. It is a force that includes and governs all others and is even behind any phenomenon operating in the universe and has not yet been identified by us.

This universal force is LOVE.

When scientists looked for a unified theory of the universe they forgot the most powerful unseen force.

Love is Light that enlightens those who give and receive it. Love is gravity, because it makes some people feel attracted to others.

Love is power, because it multiplies the best we have, and allows humanity not to be extinguished in their blind selfishness. Love unfolds and reveals. For love we live and die. Love is God and God is Love.

This force explains everything and gives meaning to life. This is the variable that we have ignored for too long, maybe because we are afraid of love because it is the only energy in the universe that man has not learned to drive at will.

To give visibility to love, I made a simple substitution in my most famous equation.

If instead of E = mc², we accept that the energy to heal the world can be obtained through love multiplied by the speed of light squared, we arrive at the conclusion that love is the most powerful force there is, because it has no limits.

After the failure of humanity in the use and control of the other forces of the universe that have turned against us, it is urgent that we nourish ourselves with another kind of energy.

If we want our species to survive, if we are to find meaning in life, if we want to save the world and every sentient being that inhabits it, love is the one and only answer.

Perhaps we are not yet ready to make a bomb of love, a device powerful enough to entirely destroy the hate, selfishness and greed that devastate the planet.

However, each individual carries within them a small but powerful generator of love whose energy is waiting to be released.

When we learn to give and receive this universal energy, dear Lieserl, we will have affirmed that love conquers all, is able to transcend everything and anything, because love is the quintessence of life.

I deeply regret not having been able to express what is in my heart, which has quietly beaten for you all my life. Maybe it's too late to apologize, but as time is relative, I need to tell you that I love you and thanks to you I have reached the ultimate answer!"

Your father Albert Einstein
(published in the 1992 book The Love Letters)

Love is the most powerful force in the entire universe—it is the same energy that binds and sustains all. It is the force from which the universe and all life is born. Love allows each of us to feel connected to not only each other but the very creation of everything that is alive. Once we understand that love is the thing that binds us to each together, we can become part of the solution instead of the problem. We can begin to truly love ourselves and one another and the planet we live on. When we live our lives in love, we become part of the universal knowledge, wisdom, gratitude, goodness and inspiration that we are all in need of. The universe is one big living organism and when you realize you are a part of that, you become aware that you are part of the Divine Wheel of Life. When you begin to understand that you are part of this master plan of unity, you begin living in your full potential and leave behind the pain, inequality, and diversion that society teaches is important. You are free to be anything you wish to be, create anything you wish to create; you are the great co-creator of your world and your experience. You are not separate but part of the unique and Divine creation of the All.

You and you alone have the choice to live in the flow of this powerful force. It is your choice at all times to feed Love or Ego consciousness, to be happy or unhappy, to be one with all creation or to battle against it. When you find yourself struggling with your life, ask yourself: "Am I struggling because I'm not what society wants me to be? Or am I struggling because I am not flowing easily with the most powerful, joyful, invigorating, life creating and universal power on earth?" Love is the most natural and most powerful emotion on earth and one of the best ways to become aligned with that flow is by knowing who you are, finding your fire, your passions and loving yourself.

Through your fire and your passion, you can create the life you wish to live. These things are very easy to talk about but much harder to live by. Right now, there are millions of refugees fleeing the Islamic State in Iraq and Syria and these people are flooding into Europe. More than a million of these refugees are arriving in Germany and many hundreds of thousands pouring into neighboring countries. As this is happening, I have heard mixed emotions from so many people. I have sat with many families living in small villages in Germany and The Netherlands that are now crowded with thousands of refugees. Many are angry or simply overwhelmed, and I can feel for them as their way of life, and their normalcy has changed so dramatically. I have also visited the makeshift shelters and housing units set up for refugees. There are some of these housing units near my home. I have also talked with these people who have fled terror with their families. It is a heartbreaking situation for everyone at this point but there is one thing that I have found to be true no matter what the case. There is no room for hate! Hate is what caused this mass destruction, chaos and heartache; and the emotion of hate will not help or solve any of it. Like I said, it is much easier to read the concept of love in a book and think: "Oh, that is nice. I want to live that way," versus having the opportunity on your doorstep to really look inside yourself and ask the question: "How can I best live in love and not live my life ruled by ego at this moment of time?"

It is very easy to feel hate or anger at the ISIS radicals and let ourselves fall into the trap of our passion ruled by ego, becoming hateful, angry, judgmental and even racist; but it is also just as easy to look at this in another way. If you are reading this book, you are probably on the path of Love consciousness—you are waking up and wanting to shift your awareness, knowing that there is a massive problem on our planet and ready to change your life for the better. The majority of you reading this book have a good home, a good job, the means to buy food and clean water, the many comforts in life including a good book to help you on your spiritual journey. We are the lucky ones; we are not the majority! We have been given great gifts and the ability to have the energy and the wellness in life to take time for our spiritual growth. Sadly, nearly half of the world's population, more than 3 billion people, live on less than $2.50 a day. Most people are shocked to find out that more than 22,000 children die EACH day due to poverty.

Living the lives we do in the western world we tend to forget how blessed we are. We live our lives and eat our food and enjoy our weekends, complain about miscellaneous nonsense and so easily judge others that we know nothing about. It is easy to fall into this trap, isn't it? We want to change the world; we want to live in a world of love and light, and it is possible for us to do that, but WE must change it. WE are the ones that have to do the work. It will not be the mother of three kids, living on a dirt floor with nothing to feed her children and a war going on outside of her front door. It will not be the father carrying his child on his back in the freezing rain trying to escape the bombs falling from the skies. It is not up to the child laborers and the enslaved women packed in overheated, overcrowded, factories working to make our H&M or Walmart t-shirts and handbags. It is not up to those trying to survive genocide by their own governments and radical groups. They are trying to survive. WE, we are the ones who need to start living in love and compassion to begin the change in this world.

There is no room for more hate in this world; there is only room for more love. We need to love each other as brothers and sisters, as human beings. We need to see each other not by the color of our skin or our religious backgrounds, but truly see each other as another image of Self. I am reminded of sitting beside a woman who was clearly upset about the refugees coming into her town. I listened for quite a while as she ranted about how: "They should go home back to their country, where they belong. They are not like us." She went on and on; the more she went on, the angrier she became; the more she tried to convince me, the more aggravated she became. I listened for a while trying to hear her out. I didn't comment on the things she said, instead I simply asked her a couple of questions. First if she had children, the answer was yes. The second question was: "If you and your children were being shot at, bombed, and hunted like prey to become sex slaves, would you run somewhere safer?" She just stared at me for a moment; she opened her mouth a couple of times but nothing came out, then she just walked away. I wasn't trying to upset her but make a simple statement. You would do anything to protect your families and loved ones, anything! No matter who you are, no matter where you come from, all people deserve goodness, kindness, safety and wellbeing! Basic human rights should be for all, not just some!

How we react in this refugee situation or any other tragic circumstances is in the choice we can make. We can either become the hate that started this mess, or we can rise above it. You can choose to resent those pouring into your little towns and become bitter and soured by the reality of the situation, or you can walk out your front door and start saying hello. We can complain about our governments not doing enough for these people, or we can clean out our attics and go visit a shelter. We can spew hate about the ISIS fighters, or we can pray for them and send them love to soften their hearts. We can literally choose how we want to express our fire in our lives; we can be passionate with love or with hate and ego.

One will burn us, and the other will bring love and warmth to all. It is a choice!

When we chose to come to this world, we came with a purpose, a reason, with a passion for who we wanted to become, what we wanted to learn and what we wanted to give. So many times I have witnessed people who have lost their passion in life, that spark that gets you up in the morning. They have forgotten why they are here. While doing personal sessions, this is one of the most asked questions: "What is my purpose?" My answer is always the same: "I don't know; only you know the answer to that." If you do not know what your passion is in life, it is time to figure it out. Literally sit down with a piece of paper and start making a list of what makes you feel good—I mean, really good, so good that tears come to your eyes, and you can feel your heart well up! We have to start remembering what makes us unique, not what makes us the same as everyone. It is a great tragedy that our schools have taught us to all fit in the same box and have molded us to be little robots. We are not the same! We are different and beautiful and gifted in individual ways. I literally get a warm fuzzy feeling all over my body just by seeing the words: Mother Earth, Wilderness, and Wildlife. My heart literally beats faster when I think of wild places I have seen on this wondrous planet. This is my absolute passion—it is who I am. I cannot and will not, ever be apart from it. It's ME, and I love it! But I know this is not what everyone feels and thinks and is passionate about. My wife Joyce has different passions in life, hers being the human body and how it all works together. We are all different, and that is how it is supposed to be.

What Is Your Passion?

What are you passionate about? What do you love? What is your fire? When I ask this to a group of people listening to one of my lectures, the one thing we are all passionate about, to some degree or another, is making the world a better place. Often I will point out that I could be giving the same talk or lecture in front of my computer at home on YouTube. It is much more comfortable to be in my pajamas and fuzzy slippers doing a recording on the computer than it is to travel, eat on the road, and sleep in someone else's bed! So why do it? The main purpose of gathering people together for a lecture is just that, to gather you all together. You see, once you know what your purpose or passion in life is, the most important thing from that moment on is to keep it burning! It is easy to be passionate about something, but if we are not using it, if we are not reassured about it, if we are not associating ourselves with it, we tend to let our fire extinguish. We human beings are funny things. We need to have reassurance now and then, and we need to feel that we are not alone. It's just the way we are; we like to belong. We like to feel that we are a part of something, and in fact, that need is what makes us so strong! The reason I do not give my lectures on YouTube is because I want to gather you all together, to show that you are not alone. There are many people like you; you just need to find each other.

One of my Elders taught me something I will never forget. He said: "think of being around a campfire, watching the red hot coals burning. What happens if I take one of the coals out and leave it alone in the dark away from the fire? What happens almost instantly to that red hot coal? It will turn black and lose all of its heat very quickly. But what happens to that same coal if I pick it up and add it back to the fire?

Within seconds, it will begin to glow red hot again." We are just like these coals in the campfire; we do need each other to burn as bright as we possibly can. On our own, we can have a little heat inside, but it is very hard to keep that heat, that personal fire inside of us going. The moment you are around others who believe like you, feel like you and are passionate like you—You will glow red hot again!

People need people; we are not a solitary species. We need each other. Instead of using our ego and our passion to hate and kill and judge we can use it to literally change the world! When you know who you are and why you sent yourself here and when you know what your passions are, you start to truly live! You can start finding people like you and growing your passions together, which is just like adding wood to a fire. The worst thing we can do is to let our fire burn out. Not because you can never get the fire back, but because it's hard to get the fire going from scratch. Many have lost their fire in the past or maybe even while reading this book you are thinking: "Oh no, what is my passion?" Or: "Oh damn...My fire is out." It is ok; it is hard to start from scratch, but it can be done. I have been with so many people who have broken down in tears, truly heartbroken because the feeling of purpose or passion has gone from their lives. If you are one of these people, dry your tears because it just needs to be found again; it is not really gone.

Most commonly, a purpose or passion is not lost, but got stuck somewhere in one way or another. I remember raising two little babies and feeling: "Where did Kiesha go?" At that time, there was no extra time or space in life for me to really live another passion. My passion became raising and being with those two little angels. A friend of mine had to take care of very sick parents, while raising two little kids and holding down a full-time job. There was no time to focus on passion or purpose other than what was in front of that person at the moment. There are many reasons why we lose focus of our passions or our purpose. The important thing to remember is that we can always get it back. The essence of who you are and why you sent yourself here to this magnificent planet will always remain inside of you. No matter how buried it can sometimes be, please remember it is still there.

The biggest issue I have found with people who feel that they are stuck in this area, is that they are projecting and believing things about themselves that are simply untrue. First, you do have a purpose and a passion; you do have fire somewhere inside of you. You just have to find it and most likely you have been looking in the wrong places. I believe very strongly that every single person on this planet is passionate about something. We all had dreams while growing up but somewhere along the line we lost perspective because the ego really set in. Something happened while growing up that scared us into hiding our dreams deep inside where it was safe from society or what someone else might have thought. We hide our passions from anyone who might crush them and we never gave these passions a chance. Maybe we never even tried to live our passion because we were too afraid we might fail, so we simply gave up. Some of us kept our passion to ourselves, because it seemed too big or too small, too normal or outrageous.

Most of the time it all comes down to "fear." Fear of not being seen, fear of what others might think, fear of rejection, fear of the unknown; fear, fear, fear! Well, let me tell you what one of the Elders once told me. Fear is only a sickness of the human mind! Indeed, fear is only a sickness of the mind. We have fear about the unknown, or what someone might think of us; so in other words we are making something up in our head. We are convincing ourselves about something that hasn't happened yet or might not ever happen. We talk ourselves into this made-up scenario, and then we feed that fear making our "story" more and more real…until BOOM: "nope, no way. I'm not going to do that. I'm not even going to try." We made up a story, panicked about it so much that we were not able to move forward. In reality, nothing has happened yet; we just made something up in our mind and then believed it.

Does this not sound like a mental illness to you? Yes, fear is a sickness of the mind. Sometimes people even panic when I ask them: "What is your passion?" As if there were a right or wrong answer to this question. Their eyes shift back and forth, and I can see the panic setting in. They start thinking: "What should I say? What's a good answer? What does she want from me? What will sound really impressive?" Be sure, there is no right or wrong answer; it is a simple question, and it should be a simple answer. What do you love? What fills your heart with joy? What are your dreams? What fills your heart truthfully?

When I ask people 'the passion question', they often think I want to hear something totally amazing, over the top and grandiose! Something that will be so profound and earth changing, something so special, they will be set apart from all others. Many times, people think that they must be a superhero in order to change the world or to be important in the eyes of others. Let me tell you, the fry cook at McDonald's is just as important and loved by Great Spirit as the Diplomat. So in finding your passion, the first thing you need to do is let your ego go for a walk and understand that you are valuable; you are good; you are unique and you do have a passion and a fire inside you. Every individual fire is just as important.

We have been taught time and time again to place value on things that do not matter. For example, when I was still living in America and just embarking on my spiritual path, I went to see a "spiritual teacher." Everyone I was associating with at the time was so excited for this teacher to come and speak. Everyone got their tickets and eventually I got on the same train of thought, knowing that this person was famous. I too jumped on the train to get a chance to see and hear this "guru".

When I arrived at the convention center, I couldn't believe the amount of people lined up waiting to go inside. There had to be a hundred people in the line. When she arrived everyone started to bow. I had never seen anything like it before in my life. The crowd was so big that when I eventually got inside I couldn't find my chair. I was a bit lost in a place so big and certainly was not used to so many people being in one room. Then this little old woman came to me and asked if she could help me to my place. She took me right up to the front and sat me down with a little pat on my shoulder and left to help others. From where I was sitting I could see back stage. I could see the "guru" surrounded by all her assistants. From between a crack in the curtain, I watched as she put her arms out to get dressed by her assistants; they dressed her in fine robes and scarves. I literally jumped out of my chair when I heard her begin to scream at one of the assistants placing one of her scarves on wrongly. The entire first three rows of people could hear her outrage very clearly. I couldn't tell what she was saying because the language she was using was not English, but anyone seeing this or hearing this must have understood the volunteer was being reprimanded. To my shock, this was not the end of it; soon I actually saw her strike another woman for placing her microphone in the wrong place.

Soon after she waved her hands for the assistants to leave her alone, she came out on stage and sat in her throne and smiled at the crowd. The lecture was about how to respect and love each other, how to give service and be humble. After the event was over the crowd went to her with such praise. Some gave her flowers; others gave money. Before you could approach her, everyone was made to bow down. It was all a bit much for me to handle, and I decided to take a leave of absence. As I was walking out of the building, I saw that same little old lady who helped me to my chair. She was walking around picking up trash that people left behind, straightening out chairs and opening the doors for people as they left the building. No one paid her any attention. She was not dressed in robes; she was not honored and adored. She was there as a volunteer, not being paid for her services, yet she was in total service. She was the exact embodiment of what the lecture was all about. She moved quickly to the door with a crooked smile and opened the door for me. I couldn't help but reach over and pull her into my arms. This was what I was looking for, this was the reason I went to the lecture: this woman was the teaching I was seeking.

That very special moment is one I will never forget. How often do we place praise, automatic attention or adoration on people because we are told to, or because everyone else does? How often do we give our attention and respect to people for the wrong reasons? How many people do we place higher than ourselves and bow down to even though we don't even know who they truly are? Our society has taught us that the small things are worthless but that status, riches and wealth are everything. I see this take place first hand every time I give a lecture or an event myself. When the lecture is over people come for a photograph, or they come to give me a hug and thank me for all I am doing. Were my gifts to the crowd any more profound than those who have donated their time and effort to make the event happen? Yes, I gave the lecture, but the event wouldn't have taken place without my wife, Joyce, taking care of each and every person in the crowd, setting up the entire event, sending the emails, taking care of tickets, the travel and lodging and making sure everyone is content.

It's true—I refuse to wear some pompous robe, and I don't have others wait on my every need. I loathe the "guru" concept. However, I too can see that people's affections and gratitude are aimed only at the one in the limelight instead of those who are in total service and get no credit for actually living by example. We have been brainwashed into thinking that those who are famous or who are in the spotlight deserve our attention and affection. For example, simply ask your children who their heroes are. The answers we tend to get back are quite frightening to be honest. Our kid's heroes are football players, pop stars, actors and actresses. Their heroes are entertainers! It is very easy to see where we place our value in this world simply by looking at a teacher's, nurses, or firefighter's monthly income compared to an entertainer's. The heroes of our children are adult men who know how to kick a ball, for crying out loud! So yes, I understand how easy it is to devalue yourself when the world around you is saying only your status and your wealth matter. It is hard to sift through all the nonsense to find your real value and hold strong to it. It is time to start loving yourself for who you really are and the good that you have inside of you; the gifts and purpose you have; the fire that lives inside you. You must do it for you; the world will not! It's time to focus on what is real, for yourself and for your kids! There is that old saying I mentioned earlier: "You cannot see the forest through the trees." Well, I think that is the exact state we are in—in our consciousness today. We are completely blind to what is going on because we are lost inside the madness.

When we look back in our history, we can see where society was clearly manipulated. However, it is not so easy to see it for ourselves today. Take, for example, the Emperor Claudius Drusus Germanicus, otherwise known as Nero. Here we have a very powerful, wealthy, spoiled, brutal, weak, erratic, extravagant, sadistic and most clearly deranged leader. We are talking about a man who had Christians rounded up, dressed in animal skins and had them torn limb for limb by wild dogs; or had them dipped in oil and lit on fire to light his gardens at night. He was a man who killed his wives and had his mother beaten to death with clubs. He was a ruler who bankrupted the empire and a murderer of all who stood in his way. He eventually burnt the entire city of Rome to the ground. Interestingly, he was also seen as a man who was loved by the people for giving them great chariot races and spectacular gladiator fights in the Colosseum; a man who threw bread to the spectators during the games. He was loved by the people because he entertained them and blinded them while doing the most unspeakable things. Are we any different? Are we too not blinded by the entertainment we are force fed daily while our leaders commit the most horrific humanitarian and ecological crimes? No matter where we look, we can find a blinding amount of brainwashing going on in our societies; from the news broadcasts teaching us that our countries actions are right and others wrong; to the magazines teaching us and our children what body image we should all have, what we should wear, how to think and how to speak and what to believe in. It is continually poured down our throats. We too are that same mass of people at the arena cheering as bread is tossed to us while the world is falling apart. It is time to stop valuing nonsense and start placing real value on who we truly are and what honorable talents and gifts we can give to the world. I want our kids to have the Jane Goodalls, the Desmond Tutus, Nelson Mandelas, David Attenborough's, the Vandana Shivas, the Sylvia Earls of the world to be our heroes; not some random entertainer.

The only way our children will learn what is right and what to stand for in this world, is by our own example. It is so imperative that we start placing value on what we stand for as human beings, our goodness, our courage and our love for each other. We must be the example; we must wake up in order to change this world and give our kids the world they deserve to live in. In order to do this we must know who we are and what we stand for; what we will tolerate and what we will not. We must know what our fire is; we must find out what our true passions are and remember why we sent ourselves here in the first place.

For decades, our indigenous leaders have been prophesying a time to come when the strongest of the strong would come to our planet. They would be the bravest of souls, who could change the outcome of the human consciousness when we found ourselves at the crossroads of destroying each other and our planet through ego. Now, with a clear and powerful voice they are saying: "You are those we have been waiting for!" We are the strongest of the strong, and we must be! We were all born to a world where the ego reigns supreme. We have been taught to use the ego in every aspect of our lives. We must be so very strong in order to realize that there is more to life—there is another way. We must change our old behavior in order to stop damaging our planet in such horrendous ways.

You would not be reading this book if you did not believe that there is another way of living than just walking blindly in the dark and destroying everything in your path. Indeed, we are the strongest of the strong; we are the prophesy come true. We are the ones that must wake up, the ones that must say: "I believe in more, in being more, and I'm going to take that first step." Our children are the change; they have come to this world with such gifts, such amazing ways of feeling and seeing the world; yet they don't quite know what to do with themselves. We label them as autistic or troubled when they cannot conform inside the box we have created for them. In truth, they ARE the change, and WE must pave a path for them in order to give them the world they deserve to learn from and grow and succeed in.

It is our generation, that must find the strength to stop the madness and start taking part in love consciousness. When we live in love and lead our lives with purpose and walk with that fire ablaze inside of us, we will clear the path for our children. We must be so very strong and Great Spirit must have such great faith in us. Remember you are great; you are powerful in who you are and the gifts you have matter! Do not let them continue to be stamped out, but rise above and stand proud of who you truly are.

List Your Passions

I want you to make a list of what you love and what your passions are. It can be anything! You like to read good books; you like to play with kids; you like to create or listen to music; you love to make people laugh. I do not care how grand or small it is, just write it down. So many times people do not think they have a passion, because what they love or find important, others will view as small…Who cares what others think! Big, small, grandiose or quiet, what you feel is important, what you love, what you find purpose in is yours! Own it! The truth is, most of us do nothing in this world to make it a better place, because we think we are too small and unseen to do any good. Well, let me ask you a question. How do you create a raging, hot fire? Do you put down a huge log and strike a match and then BOOM instant burning flames? No! How do you build a fire?

First, you gather the kindling, the little bits of dry grass that will catch a spark, then you will add thin little twigs to ensure that the fire is really burning, then small branches to make it hotter, then pieces of chopped wood and when the fire is burning really hot and really strong, you will add a log to keep it going. It is ok to start small and work your way up to that blazing fire you want inside of you. We all have the fire inside us; we just need to build it up so the flame will produce the warmth and the light that will sustain our bodies (our earth). While building that fire inside of you, always remember to live your passion through love, never through ego. In Love, your fire will burn bright without injury to yourself or others. Your passion in life doesn't have to be monumental; it doesn't have to concur global warming and be in the spotlight. It can be a simple service to others. It can be kindness in the smallest ways.

Just as easily as you can let your fire go out, you can burn yourself up. We all know someone like this in our lives. Someone who is burning too hot. Someone who honestly believes that if they talk the loudest, others will see how important they are. If they make themselves seen by throwing a fit, then things will go their way. They are the same people who are ready to fight any battle simply to prove how right, how strong and how powerful they are. There are people who have convinced themselves that they have such great gifts for the world that they stand above all others and must be recognized for their greatness. These things are made and fed by the ego. I have to admit; I have never come into contact with so many egos since becoming a spiritual teacher. It is sad to me, but so very true. I have never met so many people living in their egos under the pretense of being more "gifted" or more "special or spiritual" than others. You wouldn't believe how many people have told me they are the reincarnations of Jesus, Mary, Isis, or kings and queens. These people are the people who are looking for recognition and praise for being extra special! I have met people who feel it necessary to convince me that they literally are from inner earth, or that they are from Sirius or some other planet.

First of all, we have all lived many, many lives before this one, and we will live many, many more after this one. We have sent our sparks of the Great I Am to learn and grow in many forms, to many places. Firstly, as long as you are living this life, in this body, on this planet, you are a human being like the rest of us and you are you. Secondly, we are all here to learn and grow in this life and when this life is over, we will send ourselves on to the next test, to bigger and better things. Christ is not going to reincarnate himself into the post office clerk who has not figured out that claiming to be Christ is simply the ego screaming for attention! Too often in the spiritual world I have witnessed so many are simply trying to outdo their neighbor with their spiritual greatness. Simply put, if you are living your life trying to impress others or be seen by others, you have lost your way.

So many of us find ourselves entering the spiritual world because we are sick and tired of the way society works and what it holds valuable. We want to leave the value of titles, money, looks, fashion and fame behind us so that we can see what is truly valuable in our lives. We want to find who we really are, and we want to be loved and valued for being ourselves. Sadly, many leave the ego based society structure with the best intentions only to fall right back into it in the spiritual world.

There is no need to focus your life on being something else or someone else. This defeats the purpose of even being here on this planet. You cannot learn and grow hidden under the disguise that your ego has created for you. Only when you strip it away and say: "This is me; I am fragile; I am vulnerable; society makes me feel small and unworthy, but I feel that I am valuable, and I want to know my truth," you can start learning how great you truly are. When we strip away our egos and all the lies we have been telling ourselves to protect or hide ourselves, we can start truly appreciating who we really are and what we are capable of. I much rather listen to the woman or man who can honestly say: "I am just me; I am looking to truly love myself, although I have many issues I want to belong to something greater than what society has to offer me," than: "I am more special than anyone else; I am actually Mary Magdalena; I can see portals and I'm here to heal you with my violet flame."

We have to truly let go of the old ways of thinking— thinking that being better than everyone else makes you worth more. All of our passions and purposes are valuable; they are what make us who we are. Not one of them is better or less than another. Thinking that someone else is more valuable than another because of their "gifts" is what Ego has taught us to believe. If we value each other on a love level, those old ways of believing can start to slip away. So you start writing down your list of things that are your passions; the things that you love and things that you value yourself for. Make sure that what you are writing has nothing to do with what you want others to value you for or what you want to be seen for. This list has nothing to do with what your ego wants or what others want. This list is about what your heart feels is true for you. It would be a grave mistake to start writing down things that you want to be praised for or to be seen as special. We are all special for the things that make us us. Not the story we want others to believe. Society has taught us that those in the limelight or those who have grandiose stories to tell, hold the most value. Quite often, those who feel it necessary to project how great they are, are hiding the biggest wounds and have no idea who they really are and what their real value is as a human being. Therefore, I advise you to be true to yourself when making your list.

When making the list, first start with all the things that you truly love in this life, all the things that make your heart beat faster, including the things that make you happy or that brings you the most joy. I also want you to write down who you really are, what are the things that make you "you". Write down what you are passionate about. Before you are finished making your list, I want you to write down the answers to: "Why did I send myself to planet Earth? What do I want to learn and what are my passions and potentials in this life? What do I stand for?" And finally, "What are my gifts to the world?" Take your time and really think and feel these answers out and then write them down. When you are done, label the paper: "My Fire!" Then prepare yourself to once again go to that special place you have made for yourself outside to honor the four directions and elements.

Creating Your Sacred Circle or Medicine Wheel: Fire

When you are ready (having the paper labeled "My Fire" in your hand), go to the place where you are making your medicine wheel. The stone representing the west, the keeper of Earth and the color of black should still be in place. Slip off your shoes in reverence of Mother Earth and with deep respect for the prayers you are about to offer for the element of Fire. You are now ready to honor the East. Stand facing the stone you have placed in the west, the keeper of earth and the color of black. Leaving about four feet (120 cm) between where you stand and the stone representing west. (You can leave more or less space depending on how large or small you are going to create your medicine wheel.) On this spot, you will place your stone to represent the East, the color of red and the keeper of the Fire element.

Before we begin with our prayers and honoring the direction of the East, we must make ourselves reverent and in gratitude. Once you have chosen your place in which to stand with your paper in hand, close your eyes and prepare yourself to begin your prayers. In this moment, with your feet placed firmly on Mother Earth, realize who you are and what a blessing it is to be here; to be able to witness and take part in all that you get to experience. We will begin just as we did with the element of Earth with the breathing meditation.

Begin by breathing the color green, the color of Earth energy, up through the soles of your feet; feel this Earth energy filling your cells and nourishing every inch of you. With every breath-in move your way up through the chakras. Remember with the final breath-in to bring the energy all

95

the way up to the top of your head and on your final exhale, breathe the energy down your arms, through your hands and out through your finger tips back into Mother Earth. This creates a complete circle of energy. This step is vitally important and should be done only at the last step once you have gone through all the chakras. Notice again, when you are at your final breathes, the warm and sometimes tingling feeling in your hands and fingertips as the energy flows from your crown chakra through your hands back to Mother.

Just as we did before, we must become fully awake to the natural world around us. Shut off all your senses but for what you can feel. What it is like to have a body, to be on this planet, what it is like to be able to feel the warmth of the sun on your skin, the raindrops falling from the sky or the soil under your feet. Just take a moment to feel and be grateful. Now listen, shut off all other senses but what you can hear. Take a moment to pay attention and listen to all the life that surrounds you, from the rustling of the leaves, to the insects and birds calling out to each other, singing their songs. Nature is always speaking; we simply have forgotten to listen. Take a moment and really listen to the conversations of beauty happening all around you. Now it is time to shut off all other senses but for smell. Do you know what Mother Earth smells like? Have you ever thought about it? Do not be afraid, bend down and smell the earth, the rich dark soil, the green grass, the leaves, the trees, smell the air…, smell the fragrance of life that is all around you.

Taste the air, open your mouth and breathe in, taste the sweet air that fills your lungs, place a blade of grass into your mouth, a stone, a leaf. Take a moment to be grateful for the gift of taste. Now stand and slowly open your eyes and truly look at all the life that surrounds you! From the smallest insect to the largest tree, take it all in, look at all the splendor Mother Earth has created for you to enjoy. Look at where you get to live! Be grateful for all the life around you and become one with the place where you stand. As you stand there at the place that you are making sacred, feel all the gratitude you have for the beautiful Mother and for the gift of your body and all of your senses. Become awake, fully awake to not only yourself but also to your surroundings. Now you are ready to honor the direction of the East, your element of Fire and the color of Red.

Stand in the place that will represent the East of your Medicine Wheel with your eyes closed and feel the soles of your feet pressed to the earth. Imagine your energy connecting to the source of heat and fire that is at the core of our Mother. Breathe in that powerful energy up through your chakra system, from the soles of your feet all the way up to the top of your head and out your hands. Let the energy build up stronger and stronger. If at any time you feel that the energy is not moving or that it is stuck, simply take your time and continue to breathe in that area. As you do this practice remember to feel gratitude, gratitude for all that you are, for the opportunity to be here living this life. Be grateful for your passions in life and for your gifts to the world. Feel love for yourself, for your authenticity, for your intentions, feel love and gratitude for the fulfillment that comes from being YOU!

As you breathe in this wonderful hot, burning gratitude and passion, let it build stronger and stronger inside of yourself. Now lift your eyes to the heavens, stretch out your arms and feel the sun's warmth pouring down upon you, giving thanks and appreciation for the light and the warmth that the sun blesses our planet with. Witness all the beauty that surrounds you and the abundance of life that is given to this magnificent planet due to the gift of the light of the sun. Become aware of the incredible light spectrum we are able to see and enjoy the boundless colors and their beauty! Be thankful for each and every new day that the sun appears, giving you a new day, a new start and a new chance to be the best I Am that you can possibly be.

Feel how blessed you are to have each new day an opportunity to be a better person. Breathe in the sun's rays into your chakra system starting at the top of your head and working your way down to your feet, breathing the sun's rays out of your feet and deep into the core of Mother Earth, combining the fire from above to that which is below inside of yourself. Feel the power of gratitude growing inside you; you are the Great I am. You are a divine soul who has sent yourself here to learn and grow and to have a human experience on this beautiful Mother Earth. You have come with great gifts. You are capable of all things, and you are a spark of the ALL. You are precious, unique and above all you are YOU, an individual unlike anyone else! In your hands you hold the Paper, the list you have made of the things you love, the things you are passionate about, the things that define you.

While facing East speak aloud the things that you are passionate about, the things that bring fire into your heart. Feel, with all your love and gratitude that flame burning bright and hot inside of you. Give thanks for all that you are and all that you will represent here on Earth as a human being in this life's journey. Give gratitude for all those who have come before you. Thank the Elders of the East, the grandmothers and grandfathers, the wise ones and the teachers who have inspired you through their fire and passion. Give thanks to the fire in your life that can burn away the old and the dead debris that has kept you from being your greatest Self.

Thank the fire within for cleaning and clearing the way for you to be the best I Am that you can be. Be grateful for the fire that lives within you that makes you passionate in love, the fire that burns within your heart that makes you who you are, what you stand for and what you believe in. Thank those in your life who help you burn bright and keep your fire burning within. Ask Great Spirit and Mother Earth to help you create an everlasting fire burning within your heart so that you can become and maintain the person you want to be. Light your sage or your tobacco and offer your prayers by blowing the smoke to the direction of the East, the sun, the core of Mother Earth and to your own heart. Wash yourself in the smoke of your prayers and then kneel down to the beloved Mother and place your paper at your feet. Blow the sage or tobacco smoke over your list and feel gratitude for your fire.

After speaking your final words of your prayer, find a stone or crystal you would like to represent the direction of the East in your medicine wheel. Place the stone opposite of the stone representing the West. Place the paper "My Fire" under the stone where it will stay. (You can paint a stone with the color that the stone represents, in this case red). You can choose what you would like, as this is your medicine wheel for your own prayers. Before you leave your medicine wheel take one more moment to remember who you are, what makes you who you are and honor the good within yourself. Honor You! With these prayers in your heart, you can now step out of your spot and continue with your day knowing that you can come back here at any time to revisit the power of the East and your own powerful fire.

The Element Wind

The element Wind might be invisible, something we cannot literally grab a hold of, see or smell. However, the importance and the effects it has on our planet and in our own lives can be seen in a great many of ways. When we think of seeing the effects of wind in our lives, we can envision examples that stretch from one extreme to the other. The dancing ripples upon a water surface, the leaves and branches of a tree swaying back and forth; the tall grasses flowing like the waves of an ocean across the prairie. The wind can also be something much more destructive, like a whirling tornado or a freezing blizzard. A spiraling tropical storm can pack wind speeds of over 160 miles/h (257 km/h) and unleash more than 2.4 trillion gallons (9 trillion liters) of rain. These invisible forces are all around us every moment of every day, no matter how subtle or how ferocious they might be.

The wind can be playful, gentle, soothing, cooling and calming, and it can just as easily be an extremely destructive, turbulent, generating unpredictable power. It is not an element you can hold in your hands, nor smell or touch. It is not an element that you can see or something that anyone can capture or train. The wind is the great harmonizer of the atmosphere. It is able to transport moist, heat, greenhouse gases and pollutants across vast distances of the globe. It can bring a fresh sweet smell of flowers in the summer and chill you to the bone in winter. It is capable of being strong enough to push and pull huge sailing ships across the oceans and rip entire buildings off of their foundations. No matter how calm or how violent the wind is, the one thing we know for sure is that it is undeniably imperative to life on our planet.

When we think of the elements, wind is not usually the one that sticks out in our mind. We tend to ignore it completely, or we complain about its presence because it's too windy outside. Let's be honest, not many of us step outside into the wind and think: "Oh good, the wind is blowing!" Perhaps we fail to appreciate the wind because we do not truly understand how vital it is to each of us and to the circle of life on our planet. So the first measure we need to take in understanding the wind element is to truly comprehend what wind actually is, how it is formed and why it is absolutely necessary on this planet.

Wind can be best described as air in motion. It is created by uneven heating of the earth's surface by the sun and because our planet's surface is made of water and land formations, it absorbs the sun's heat unevenly. As the sun heats up the surface of the earth, the atmosphere also warms. Some areas of our planet receive uninterrupted sunlight all year round and are always warm, like the equator. Other places receive indirect sunlight, so the climate is cooler. Warm air, which weighs less than cold air, rises. Cool air then moves in and replaces the rising warm air. This movement of cooling and warming air is what makes the wind blow. We also know that all air contains water vapor. When the warm air rises and expands, it is soon cooled and cool air cannot hold as much water vapor as warm air. Some of that water vapor connects onto minuscule little pieces of dust that are floating around in the air forming into a droplet of water. When millions and millions of these little droplets come together they form a cloud and as we all know without clouds, there is no rain, and without rain life wouldn't be as we know it.

One of the most amazing examples of this can be seen

right in front of your eyes like in Cape Town, South Africa on
Table Mountain. If you have been there yourself, you know
what I am talking about. It's truly breathtaking to stand on
a mountain and watch the clouds form over the ocean and
slowly rise up over the top of you, then slope back down the
mountain top. Another great place to see this taking place is in
Lima Peru, a very, very dry place with a vast desert stretching
as far as the eye can see but as you stand at the coast, you can
watch the clouds form thick in the sky and then melt away
as fast as they came. Although these clouds do not form into
a rainstorm, the process itself is truly incredible to witness.

We can also see it taking place in the great jungles and
rainforests around the green belt of our planet. Witnessing
vast amounts of moisture rising up from the canopy and
forming enormous rain clouds is a wondrous experience.
However, understanding the true gift of wind for the survival
of our rainforests is truly mind blowing. Did you know that
without the wind, our rainforests simply couldn't contain
the abundance of life that we know it to have? When you
think of the elements in the Amazon rainforest, I doubt you
would think of the wind, but without the wind blowing in
from hundreds and hundreds of miles away, the rainforest
wouldn't receive the fertilizer and nutrients that it depends
on to survive. Over 182 million tons of dust from the
Sahara desert is carried by huge wind storms to the Amazon
rainforest. The dust brought from the Sahara contains the
much-needed phosphorus, travels deep into the jungle which
then acts as a fertilizer for the flora and fauna living in the
forest. Phosphorus is essential to all plants; most of all to
those in very wet climates where it is washed away due to the
constant rain which causes continual run off into the streams
and out of the forest. How fascinating is it to know that

without the sand storms from the Sahara desert, our Amazon rainforest wouldn't exist!

Speaking of the Sahara desert, I am reminded of one of the trips I took to Egypt, where Joyce and I were able to experience the power of the wind in several different ways. One of the most astounding and a bit silly memories was of being on the Nile river cruise. It was over 40 degrees Celsius, and we literally couldn't walk barefooted on the deck of the boat or our feet would burn almost instantly. So there we were in our swimming suits and socks standing in the shade of the deck overhang in all our fashion glory debating who would run out into the sun first to get in the pool. I lost the debate of course and had to go first. Have you ever tried to run tip toed in socks on a super-heated, very glossy wooden ship deck before? Well, let's just say it's not easy nor is it attractive! Not until we were both in the water did we notice we were the only two outside on the deck of the boat and the sky was starting to turn a dark orange. That's when we looked behind us and saw a wall of sand blowing towards us. It was beautiful and luckily for us; it was far out enough that we could take a moment to really enjoy the colors and the immensity of the sand storm. It looked like huge pillowy clouds of rolling sand moving in from the desert with the most beautiful colors of orange I have ever seen.

We got up out of the water deciding that perhaps we should go back in like all the other smart people who were on the same boat. It was no more than 20 steps from the pool to the stairway where we could enter the lower deck of the boat, but in those 20 steps our swimming suits had completely dried. Being in that hot wind was literally like standing in front of a giant hand dryer. I can honestly say I have never experienced wind like this before. As the days went by and we finished our tour down the Nile we were greatly blessed to spend some time with the Bedouin people out in the desert. We cooked our meals outside in the dunes on open fires. We sang and danced with them under the night sky, and we laughed and screamed as they drove us straight up and down towering sand dunes. One of my favorite parts of the trip with them was experiencing the White and Black deserts.

To be with the Bedouin people, so far from civilization in such an ancient and almost magical place, left me truly speechless. It was like being on the moon; the landscape was literally unlike anything I had ever seen before. The Black Desert was a rugged land with towering crumbled mountains made of tough jagged black volcanic rock. The sand was coarse and packed hard and there was a sense of a deep sleeping, ancient energy, something hard to explain in words. To be honest I do not believe I have ever felt the energy of Mother Earth like this before. The White Desert, on the other hand, was soft, gentle and altogether a different feeling. The landscape almost glowed from the pure white powdery sand against the blue sky. The White Desert looked like a still ocean rolling out into the distance with standing white lunar looking formations marooned and left to wither away in the wind. These chalky white formations appeared as if they defied gravity, standing alone, almost hovering in the mirage of heat waves against the sand. It was very striking to see what the wind could do, knowing that these singular standing formations were once part of a 100 meter tall plateau.

Wind literally is an element of creation. It can wither away the most hardened stone, erode and sculpt the most amazing natural wonders in the world. It is able to carry sand and volcanic ash for thousands of kilometers around the globe distributing fertilizer to the soil, spreading seeds to repopulate our forests, jungles and grasslands. It can cause the most destructive storms that devastate entire communities in the form of tornadoes, hurricanes, massive waves and intense erosion of farmlands and ancient buildings. The wind is a very powerful element that can be a destroyer or a creator and has often been viewed as a God or Deity in many cultures. Whether it is the Hindu God of wind Vayu, Pauahtuns the wind Deity of the Maya, or Amun God of creation and wind from ancient Egypt; you can find creation stories, legends and myths as well as deep respect and honor towards the element of wind as a great creator and destroyer of things.

The Native Americans have many names for wind spirits and gods such as Koko-u'hthe', Cyclone storm spirit from the Shawnee, or Tate, the Wind God of Lakota mythology that tells of a legendary figure named whirlwind woman or "Huupiriku'su." She was a very powerful wind spirit from the Northern Plains tribes, who could be dangerous at times in her natural force and strength, but she was not hostile or malicious in any way. Rather, she was an unstoppable force of nature who brought spiritual gifts and visions to worthy people. In some traditions, she has been viewed as the spirit of the tornado, while in others, she was a human girl who turned into Whirlwind Woman after being swept up by a tornado.

In the Japanese culture, the element of Wind is called Fu. It represents things that grow and expand. Wind is viewed as the energy of movement and breath. It is also associated with being open-minded and carefree as well as with other personalities or traits of being wise, experienced, compassionate and having a free spirit. In the Chinese culture and medicine, wind is represented as Feng. In the Orient, the word for wind is often associated in relation to health and disease. In ancient Chinese medical texts of Lingshu, the eight winds were related to the eight directions. In the Tao Te Ching the Chinese sage Lao Tzu says: "Tao is the breath that never ends. It is the mother of all creation." The words Prana, (Sanskrit) and Bindu (Tibetan) express the life-principle; the breath of life; energy.

I have always been in awe of the power of the wind. In my early twenties I packed my backpack, jumped in my old CJ-7 jeep and headed out to explore a large outcrop of boulders near the mountain we called Flat Top in the San Luis Valley. Earlier that year I had heard of two boys from my town having found a small cave inside the boulders which were covered in Native American hieroglyphs. I wanted to see this for myself! I had searched and searched every nook and cranny that I could find looking for an entrance into the rocky outcrop but never found a cave. I did, however, find more than one rattle snake den and figured I should probably stop searching before I got bit. I reluctantly gave up and decided to find a spot atop one of the highest boulders to have a bit of lunch when the wind began to really pick up. At first, it was just a cold steady wind that I was used to that time of year, but soon the wind became so strong I was unable to keep the hood of my jacket on, much less finish my meal. I stood up to leave when a huge gust of wind literally picked me up and threw me down several feet away from where I was initially standing. I got back up and had a laugh to myself then pushed my body into the wind in order to stand up right. It was an exhilarating feeling, and for some reason, I decided to inch my way up to the edge of the great boulder. I specifically remember having a conversation with "Mother", telling Her that I trusted Her then leaned my entire body over the edge and closed my eyes. With tears streaming from the corners of my eyes due to the absolute pressure of the wind and only the tips of my toes still touching the rock beneath me, I was held in limbo over the edge of the rock cliff. I do not know how long I was there, but I will always remember the amazing power of the wind that held me safe. It was not the smartest thing to do, but it was an absolute spiritual experience and incredibly thrilling. Thinking back on this, I still to this day do not know if those boys were just pulling my leg, or if they really did find a cave with hieroglyphs.

I am sure we all have a memory about the wind, maybe not hanging off a rocky cliff but perhaps watching the leaves blow, or being on a sail boat as it drifts across the water. The Wind element is something that should be respected and revered as a powerful creator. Understanding why our planet needs wind and knowing how the element of Wind affects the world we live in, we must ask ourselves: "How does wind represent itself for us, the human being?"

The Wind element represents itself for each of us in the form of speech. There are millions of life forms on this planet, yet we, the human beings, are the only ones who have been given the gift of speech. Our words are powerful and just like the element of Wind on our planet, we can create massive destruction to ourselves and others or create with it. We can use our speech to either erode away and destroy one another's self-esteem and self-worth, or we can spread the seeds of love and compassion, acceptance and joy and knowledge. We have free will and choice to either use our words to belittle, aggravate, humiliate and devastate or to help create, fertilize, and grow green again the good, the positive and uplifting consciousness for ourselves and our fellow brothers and sisters.

If you have ever listened to me giving a lecture or a workshop, you most likely have heard me say on several occasions: "Your words create the world you choose to live in." A simple example of this is to imagine yourself walking down the street and the first person you encounter you choose to say something rude to. Do you think they will say something polite and kind back to you, or say something just as rude? It is true, what you say and with what intention you say those words, will come right back to you. We create the world we live in with every action and the words we choose to speak. Most of the time we are not even aware of our words. We are not conscious of what we are actually creating. We are just living our lives without knowing if we are feeding love consciousness or ego consciousness.

Challenge

Some time ago, I decided to set a challenge for myself and just see how many times my words or my emotions were positive or negative throughout the day. I have to say, by the end of that day I was really shocked at the outcome.

The day began with me failing miserably at my own 'positivity test' the moment the alarm went off. Now, I don't know about you, but my first words after hearing the dream killing, eardrum piercing sound of the alarm, are not very positive. I am not even sure if my first reaction to the alarm was an audible word, more of a groan or aggravated mumble. Let's just say it was not positive, nor expressing love and light! So the first points of the days went to the negative box of my 'positivity-test'. I made my way down the stairs where there is always a very excited Labrador wagging his tail and waiting to be taken outside. Pushing past him, still rubbing my eyes awake, I fumbled around for my shoes and socks to notice there was only one sock. The renowned sock eating dog was now sitting by the back door with a guilty look on his face trying not to make eye contact. So with only one sock and a pair of rain boots on I made my way through the kitchen to let him out when I notice the mess. My son had used every pan, knife and fork as well as the entire content of the fridge to make himself his school lunch. There were dirty dishes in the sink and outside, there was a lawn that needed to be mowed for several weeks. The floor needed moping; I had a client coming to the house in one hour, and I only had one sock on! Let's just say the negative expression of the day was outweighing the positive that morning: I failed my 'positivity-test'. I think we all have had days like this. Actually, I imagine most of our days are like this. However, the key is to catch ourselves in the negative and change it into the positive. That night as I lay in bed mulling over how epically I failed this challenge, I realized it was truly my own choice in which light I wanted to see the circumstances I was in. The next morning the alarm went off, and NO, I did not have an overwhelming sense of peace and excitement, but I did catch myself and turned my negative into a positive. I took a moment to be grateful for the new day I was being given here on this beautiful planet. I got up and walked down the stairs and patted my beautiful dog on his head and thought to myself how wonderful it is to share my life with an animal that I get to love and receive love from every day. I walked into the kitchen and assessed the damage and had to smile. Yes, it was a mess, but it was my mess. I am blessed with a beautiful home that gives us shelter and safety; I have a kitchen and a fridge with plenty of food in it to feed my family. I have a wonderful home with a green garden in a kind little town. Yes, the lawn needs to be mowed, but it can wait. I can spend my time worrying and complaining about everything I have to do or I can choose to be grateful for all that I get to do.

I was astonished at the outcome of this little test I took for myself. I believed I was being, thinking and speaking positive, but I surprised myself when I started paying attention to how I was experiencing my reality. I think it is the same for a lot of us. We do not stop to think about the things we say or the words we use; we are just on automatic pilot. Words have a monumental power in our everyday lives. They give us the possibility to express and communicate our experiences with each other. Most of us don't even realize that the words we are automatically or constantly choosing to use, also affect what we experience.

It is time to realize that you can take control over your habitual use of words and change the almost automatic negative expressions of life into something positive. By understanding that your words have power and create the life you are experiencing, you can almost instantly change how you think, feel and see the way you live your life.

So I challenge you to choose a day and take the 'positivity-test' for yourself and evaluate your thoughts and words. Are they negative or positive? How are they affecting you and those around you?

We often do not realize how powerful our words can be, especially for children. As children, we are like little sponges, accepting and holding onto the words and emotions that someone instilled upon us. We all have been molded to some degree by the adults around us and their opinions, their actions, education, their understandings of the world, economy, race and culture. We absorbed the ideas of parents, family members, teachers and friends as to who we were and who we wanted to become. We were all put into an educational system at some point and taught to believe that we were either the smart kid or the dumb one, the pretty or ugly kid, the good or the bad child. We lived our lives in this perpetual way of thinking about ourselves; all because of what someone else said to us. If we don't wake up out of this mindset, we will end up living our lives dictated by what others have said about us. Even as adults we tend to believe that we are good if someone else gives us praise. Without even knowing that we have done it to ourselves, we are living our lives and convincing ourselves that somebody's opinion of us is true. We are not great because someone says we are; we are not bad because someone says we are. The expressed opinion of others is not who you are. Still, how many of us define ourselves by these opinions? Our words can do great harm and they can do great good. We must remember our words are extremely powerful!

Throughout our history, we can see where individuals like Nelson Mandela, Shivaji Bhonsle, Martin Luther King Jr. and Harriet Beecher Stowe, used the power of words to bring back a dignity and self-worth to the masses. By truly believing in something and using their wind to spread their seeds of passion, they have changed the lives of many. Sadly, I believe it is much easier for us to think of names of people who have used their words to influence the masses in the most horrific ways. Our history books and films are filled with war stories, evil leaders, invasions, the holocaust, witch hunts, the crusades, Muslim conquests, Mongol invasions and the Ottoman wars. The list can go on and on. Within seconds we can all name three or four terrible tyrants who used their voice to convince the masses to hate and wage war against another group of people. The saddest thing to me is that it is usually done in the name of "God." Every single war ever waged on this planet (whether it be because of politics, money, economics or religion) has been started because of one individual's ability to instill a powerful belief and emotion in many through words.

Our words can be used to either create or destroy. The power of speech is one of the greatest gifts we were ever given as human beings. Not only can we use this great gift to express ourselves in an array of emotions, insights and intuitions; we can also use speech to heal ourselves and others. I am sure most of you have heard of the brilliant Japanese author, researcher and scientist Dr. Masaru Emoto. Mr. Emoto spent his life devoted to helping others understand the power of prayer, emotions and words through the use of water. Through his research, we can literally witness the power of our words over the minute crystals inside particles of frozen water. I will explain more about this research in the chapter: The Element of Water.

The power of our words can also be seen in EFT (Emotional Freedom Techniques), which use tapping on certain meridian points while making positive statements. It is also known as "psychological acupressure." The technique works by releasing certain blockages in the energy systems. There are many other ways the voice can heal, calm, energize, uplift and motivate, through music, meditation, toning, song, and even hypnosis. When it comes to the power of words, the ways to heal ourselves are limitless.

Out of all the personal healing sessions I have done, working with peoples' blockages in life, over 90% of those blockages have to do with the throat chakra. We as a whole have a problem with expressing ourselves. We do not feel entitled to express our emotions. This can lead to all sorts of mental, emotional and even physical illnesses. The biggest problem I have seen is that we do not feel we are allowed to express our true desires, our passions and our belief in Self. We have been trained by our societies to express ourselves in a certain way or to simply be silent in many cases. Women's voices throughout history have been belittled, unheard, dismissed, ignored or simply silenced. Men, on the other hand, have always been expected to be strong, upfront, demanding, powerful and assertive. Men were not allowed to be soft, gentle and unguarded, because this would make them look weak. We have to let go of this old world stigmata and start speaking with true intention and with our true passion.

Take, for instance, a woman receiving a compliment about something she is wearing. The first thing she will say back to the person giving her the compliment is most likely going to be a dismissal of the compliment. "Oh, this old thing?" "No, I don't know; it doesn't make me look too fat?" Or, it is responded to by saying an automatic compliment back without thought: "Oh, you too, I really like your shirt." In truth, the whole conversation is nonsense, if you do not really feel or think it in all honesty. In America, the number-one way of greeting each other is: "Hi, How are you?" Followed by the answer, "Good, How are you?" None of which we really meant or really want an answer to. I hadn't even realized I was doing it until coming to live in The Netherlands and greeted people in this way and actually received an uneasy explanation of how their day was going. While in the UK, they like to greet someone by saying: "Are you alright?"; which took me a little while to figure out I didn't look like something was wrong with me; it was just their way of saying hello (I hope).

The point being, we all have these automatic sayings and replies and hardly ever actually express our genuine interest or feelings. Most of us do not even know what our true sound or our true voice sounds like. I am not talking about your voice when singing a song or listening to yourself speak on camera. I'm talking about your true, raw emotional sound. Have you ever allowed yourself to scream? To yell at the top of your lungs? To express your true raw emotional sound?

There are two types of people that have a very imbalanced throat chakra. The first type of person is so caught up in their own voice and their own wishes and their own ego that they will bulldoze anyone around them to be heard and to be right. We all know someone like this. The person that always speaks the loudest in the room, the one that will speak until others agree with them or make a scene if they are not heard and agreed with. The second type of person is someone who will sit back and become more and more quiet. They are the ones who are too afraid to stand up and say how they really feel, even when it comes to doing the right thing. These people are too afraid to express their true emotions and end up swallowing their pain and emotions, which can cause mental, emotional and physical problems later on in life.

For those with the overpowering need to be heard and seen, I simply say this: "Your voice is important but your ego is not." For those who cannot find their voice I say: "It is time to find it." There is an important practice to finding your true sound, your raw voice and that is to scream and to yell (at the appropriate time and place, mind you). So your first assignment for the Wind element is to find your voice. I want you to pick a place outside where you can be as loud as you want to be, or a place in the house with a nice insulated pillow. Once you have found your spot, I want you to feel first and foremost that you have the right to do this, that your voice does matter, that you do not have to be silent. I want you to find your power, find your fire, your passion inside of yourself. Find whatever part of your Fire element needs to be expressed, whether it is pain, guilt, anger or empowerment, joy, bliss, love. Whatever it is that wants to come out, I want you to feel this emotion as much as you possibly can feel. Let it engulf you; make it as real and as powerful as you can. When this feeling, this fire has built itself up into that raging volcano, that blistering heat, then open your mouth and let your raw and powerful voice be heard. This should be a sound, not a word, not an expression, not a song or a melody; this should be your true sound! Do it until you feel your fire, your passion and emotion has expelled itself. Allow yourself to really let go and begin to open up your throat chakra— give your voice the power of the wind.

You can be the most passionate person in the world, but without voice, you cannot bring those passions to life; just as a fire cannot burn without the air. The only way to make a fire hotter and hotter is to give it oxygen. The way to have a fire burn itself out is to deprive it of air. Are you giving voice to what you are passionate about? Are you spreading the seeds of your dreams, hopes, beliefs and purpose? Or are you letting the fire burn out inside of you? Remember that with your words, you can either create a negative world for yourself or a positive one. As children, we are those sponges that absorb what others tell us to believe about ourselves, but as adults we have the ability to choose. We can accept what others tell us to believe about ourselves or we can say: "No, I do not accept this for myself." Ultimately, it is your choice to be the person you want to be. It is your choice to choose how you want to express yourself and what you want to create.

You can be the grouchy girl with one sock on standing in the messy kitchen, or you can be the girl with one sock on, in the mess, absolutely loving the life she has. It is all your choice.

Creating Your Sacred Circle or Medicine Wheel: Wind

Now it is time for us to once again make our way to the area in which you want to create your Sacred Circle or Medicine Wheel representing the four directions and elements. Before you begin, please do the Earth Breathing Meditation (see page 55) to balance your chakras. Take a few moments to awaken yourself to all your senses and the life that is around you on this beautiful planet. Close your eyes and take the time to listen to all the life around you. Feel the elements on your body, taste the air, the grass, breathe in and smell the earth. Then open your eyes and look at the magnificence that surrounds you. Feel how magical this life is and how blessed you are to be on this beautiful planet and to walk this journey. When you have connected with the Mother your own energy begins to rise by standing with your bare feet touching the ground and facing the direction of the South on your medicine wheel.

At this point, we will begin giving thanks and reverence to the direction of the South and the color yellow, which represents the element of the wind. Now you can light your sage or burn tobacco and offer it to the South, to all the Elders, the grandmothers and grandfathers and the ancient wisdom that has been taught and is being taught from our indigenous peoples in the South. Honor the warm winds that blow, which bring us all manner of plant life, our fruits and vegetables; honor the winds that blow our seeds and pollens from place to place. Give gratitude for your own voice and the power that it carries. Sing a song from your heart, tone or chant to the direction of the south and let the air carry your prayers. Express your prayers of hopes and your joys, chant and give voice to you pains and let the wind carry it away to heaven and earth and all that is in-between. Let your prayers and your expression be heard, let your wind carry your passions into the air with the sage and tobacco.

When you are finished with your prayers, honor the element of Wind, the direction of the South and the color of yellow by placing a stone of your choice where your feet are on the medicine wheel. Then close the prayers by blowing the smoke of tobacco, infused with your prayers and your wind over the stone. Remember how powerful your words are and choose them carefully; they have the power to create or to destroy.

The pessimist complains about the wind;
The optimist expects it to change;
The realist adjusts the sail.

– William Arthur Ward

The Element Water

Water is, without a doubt, the most important resource in the world and our home is a very watery place. We often call our beautiful Mother Earth the Blue Planet considering 71% of Her surface is covered by water, and Her oceans consist of about 97% of all the water on Earth. The oceans are the largest ecosystems on the planet; they are the Earths' largest life-supporting complex network. The oceans of the world contain around a million different species and provide a sixth of the animal protein eaten by humanity. They hold the answers to new medications for many diseases. They absorb carbon dioxide from the atmosphere, regulate our planet's temperature, create our weather patterns; and thanks to a tiny little organism called phytoplankton, oceans create most of the oxygen we breathe. Our oceans are vital to survival of humankind. With that in mind, it is incredible that we understand more about the surface of the moon than we do about our own oceans. There is so much we do not comprehend, so many species we have not even encountered yet. It is exciting to think of all that is still to be discovered about our precious and diverse waters.

Water is never sitting still. Thanks to the water cycle, our planet's water supply is constantly moving from one place to another and from one form into another. Whether it is the water vapor in the air, the water in lakes and rivers, the icecaps and glaciers or underground aquifers, our fresh water supplies are always on the move. The journey often starts on a mountain top, the snow melt makes its way down little channels and as it grows from humble streams to mighty rivers, it builds in power, creating rapids. The water becomes low in nutrient but very high in oxygen. This clean and most important resource is a pure gift from Mother Earth; most life on this planet cannot live without it. The earth's water is constantly circulating itself; snow melts into our rivers; our rivers water our crops; the runoff goes back into the waterways or eventually evaporates back into vapor in the air; where it will recycle itself into rain and then fall down again. Many of us do not realize that the water here on Mother Earth today is the same water that existed during the time of the dinosaurs. Our water does not leave our planet; it simply recycles itself. Therefore, it is so important for us to keep our waters clean and unpolluted—it is all we have!

Without water, our human bodies simply couldn't function; it is absolutely essential for our survival. Water regulates our body temperature, moistens our eyes, mouth and nose, lubricates our joints, protects our organs and tissue, and flushes waste. It helps dissolve minerals and nutrients to make them accessible for the body to use and carries oxygen to the cells. Did you know that your brain is composed of about 80 percent of water? Our bodies simply must have water to survive. We can on average live without food for around a month, but we can only survive 5-7 days without drinking water. Now, most of us know we need water to survive. However, I don't think you know how much water you use on a daily basis. When we are asked: "How much water do you use every day?" We think of what we drink or how long our shower was; in reality we all use a lot more water than we think. If we start to think about the meals we ate that day, what means of transportation we took, the cleaning we did, we can start to get a better understanding of how much water we actually use. Studies show that on average 6,800 gallons (25,741 liters) of water is required to grow one day's food for a family of four. 6.800 Gallons of water just to grow our food for one meal! That does not include the water we use to clean the food or wash the dishes after we eat. Take, for example, the following: Did you know that it takes 20 gallons (75 liters) of water to make one pint of beer? Or that it takes 2,500 gallons (9,464 liters) of water to produce one pound of beef? Or that 477 gallons (1,805 liters) of water are required for 1 pound of eggs? Or that it takes 1,000 gallons (3,785 liters) of water to produce 1 gallon of milk? It is shocking at first to realize how much water we use on a daily base. We need water for so many reasons, not just for our typical daily shower and glass of water.

Any of us can take a few minutes to look around our homes and begin to get a pretty good idea of how important water is. Not just for the potted plant in the window, but for every natural fibered material in our home, from the curtains, sofa, and kitchen table to the products in our fridge, the energy behind every outlet and the fuel that is in our car. Every stitch of clothing you have on including the rubber soles on your shoes—water has made it possible! Most of us do not think about the use of water when we flip a light on, but did you know that keeping a single ordinary 60 watt light bulb on for 12 hours uses as much as 60 liters of water? According to the researchers at the Virginia Water Resources Research Center, our thermoelectric power plants use more than 500 billion liters of fresh water a day in the United States alone, which roughly translates to 95 liters water to produce 1 kilowatt hour of electricity. Water is used to pump the crude oil out of the ground then used to remove the pollutants from the power plant exhaust. Furthermore, it generates the steam that turns the turbines; it flushes away the residue after the fossil fuels are burned and cools the plant while it is being used.

Many of us turn to Bio Fuels thinking it is better. A big shocker is that to produce enough soybean based biodiesel to give power to a home for one month. Biodiesel will consume more than 180,000 liters water to irrigate the soil of a soybean crop. There is no getting around it; we use vast quantities of water in our everyday lives. We need water. We will always need water, but there is not a great amount of clean or fresh water on our planet—so we must honor, protect, value and not waste the fresh water we have.

Knowing that a lot of our water has become polluted we automatically turn to bottled water thinking that this is the best solution. Is this true? Now, I am not talking about the areas on our planet that lack clean water. I am talking about the average American or European who thinks it is classy to have a bottle of water rather than tap water. Is it the right choice? Why do we do it? In most cases bottled water is less regulated than tap water. Even in taste tests across the globe people tend to choose tap water over bottled water. Bottled water companies say they are just meeting consumer demands, but who would demand a less desirable, less sustainable, more expensive product that you can get basically for free from your tap? Bottled water costs about 2000 times more than tap water. It is incredible; Americans alone buy over half a billion bottles of water every week. That is enough plastic bottles to circle the globe 5 times. And do you know where over 1/3 of our bottled water comes from? The tap! It gets even crazier. Did you know the amount of oil it takes to make the water bottles used by Americans for a year, could fuel over a million cars? So just think of all the energy and resources it takes to make the plastic bottle, to ship it around the world, to market it and sell it to us, the consumer, who drinks it in a couple of minutes and then throws it directly into the trash can. The story gets even worse. Over 80% of these water bottles are dumped into landfills where they will sit for thousands of years or they will be burned, releasing the toxic pollutants into our air. If the water bottles do not end up on our landfills, they are thrown out into the ocean dumps where they will slowly breakdown into smaller pieces. These micro plastics are then being consumed by animals. Big corporations that produce bottled water (with that pretty little image of a mountain or a tropical plant on the label) are actually billion dollar industries that give us a product less desirable than the tap water we can get out of our own faucets. We need to step out of the blind marketing frenzy and hypnosis of advertisement and start taking a good look at what we are actually doing. One third of what the world spends on bottled water in one year, could pay for projects providing clean water to everyone in need; that is a huge number when you think of the 780 million people lacking access to an improved water resource! When we become conscious of what we are doing, we can actually make a change in our unconscious behavior. We need to think before buying a bottle of water. There is no need to buy bottled water again and again when we can have a reusable and Bio friendly bottle that is refillable from the tap.

Water provides us our food, our oxygen, our homes, our clothes and even our bodies. Knowing this, we should honor, respect and protect the water of our planet with great passion. The Indigenous Elders have been telling us for decades that soon clean water will be more highly valued than gold. Today, I believe we can see that coming true as our waterways are becoming more and more polluted and misused; not just by oil spills in our oceans or horrific disasters like the Japanese

Fukushima nuclear reactor plant (that is to this day pouring out over 300 tons of radiation into the Pacific, now circulating worldwide); there are also the toxic runoffs into our fresh water systems; the use of water for our animal agriculture is the leading cause of species extinction, water pollutants, and habitat destruction.

Industrial agriculture uses over 70% of the world's fresh water supply; the water polluted by these agricultural farms can destroy entire ecosystems and become toxic to humans, plants and animals alike. Massive livestock farms create huge cesspools that store the animal waste. These lagoons often leak into adjacent waterways which become polluted with harmful bacteria, nitrates, and dangerous microbes that cause outbreaks of disease, massive fish die-offs and dead zones for life. In addition to the colossal water pollution, animal agriculture creates enormous habitat destruction by clear cutting forests for grazing or to convert the land into crops for feeding livestock. Subsequently, come in the herbicides, chemical fertilizers and pesticides that poison the waterways. The habitat loss for indigenous species is monumental, causing catastrophic numbers of animals to become endangered or even go extinct.

Greenpeace Brazil announced their report to the World Social Forum stating that at present over 80% of the deforestation of the Amazon basin is due to cattle ranching. This is staggering and heartbreaking for many reasons; not only because of the unprecedented loss of animal and plant life; it also causes uprooting of indigenous peoples. Furthermore, the forest that we destroy provides us with 20% of the oxygen we breathe every year and it gives us fresh water that falls as rain. Each canopy tree transpires up to 200 gallons (757 liters) of water annually. That means one acre of land in the rainforest produces 20,000 gallons (75,708 liters) of water into the atmosphere, creating clouds and rain. When the forests are clear-cut we lose those vital trees that provide the world with oxygen and rain; the land becomes dry and brittle, unable to hold moisture as the cattle trample and take every last bit of vegetation away. Furthermore, the water that is left is being polluted. We can look at factory runoff, agricultural farming and oil spills and we can also at the smaller things like not fixing that leaky faucet, leaving a light on too long or not picking that piece of trash up out of the river. One thing is always certain: wherever there is neglect of the water, everything and everyone will suffer. When we think about the purpose and importance of water on our planet, it is easy to understand how vital it is to all life. What is not always as easily understood is how the element Water represents itself inside of us, the human being. I am not simply speaking about how our bodies are 70% water. I am looking for an answer on a more spiritual level of knowing. When it comes to fully understanding the water element in our lives, we must also understand crystals.

Crystals

Crystals are fascinating, seemingly magical and beautiful formations of Mother Earth, ranging in many different colors, shapes and sizes. Now the question is: why are crystals so important? To fully understand this question, we have to take a look at the new and exciting discoveries being made the last couple of year and we must reawaken the ancient knowledge about crystals from our distant past.

Thanks to Nikola Tesla, we know that all things in the universe are forms of energy and that everything in this universe has its own vibration and frequency, that includes crystals. Furthermore, it is possible for one form of energy to affect another. All things are energy; all things have a vibration, and some energies are stronger than others. Many of you have heard me say: "The strongest energy always wins." This is a universal truth. With this knowledge, you can use crystals to heal, clean, align and energize, even alter the vibrations of the body chakras and cells.

There is monumental evidence showing that our ancient ancestors knew a great deal about the energetic, emotional, physical and spiritual uses of crystals. We know that the ancient Egyptians used an array of crystals for spiritual insight, protection, healing the body and mind. The most intriguing to me is the amount of crystals in the building blocks of the pyramids themselves and the majority of obelisks constructed out of granite, a stone containing high concentrations of energy-responsive quartz crystal. Quartz has the ability to convert the Earth's natural electrical vibrations into usable energy, because of its crystalline structure. We know that the Great Pyramid contains huge amounts of quartz crystal. A very interesting finding is that the Great Pyramid, along with the obelisks around the world make up a global network of energy-using crystal. It sounds perhaps farfetched but if we begin to study more recent free energy ideas; we come across Nicola Tesla again, who used the same concept of creating free energy-using crystals.

In July 1899, Nicola Tesla announced he had invented a way to transmit electricity through the air by harnessing the Earth's natural conductivity. His key component for this system of limitless amounts of electricity was the use of quartz crystal. If Tesla could do it in the late 1890's, why not the ancient Egyptians? We are finding more and more evidence that our ancestors were very complex and highly intelligent people. The ancient Sumerians were the first people having a historical record of using crystals in what they called "Magic Formulas." We also have the ancient Greeks, whose word for "crystal" means "ice," believing that clear quartz was frozen ice that remained solid. The ancient Greek word for Amber is electron; one of the most fascinating things about Amber is that when rubbed, it becomes electrical charged. Therefore, the word electricity derives from the word Amber, or electron as the ancient Greeks like to call it. The ancient Chinese incorporated the use of healing crystals including crystal tipped needles for acupuncture and Pranic healing sessions. Roman, Japanese, Maori, Native American, South American, Mexican, and Indian Cultures were all using crystals in one form or another. We have a profound history of using stones and crystals, all the way back to our prehistoric roots. Our ancient ancestors possessed a vast knowledge of crystals and those crystals played a major role in their existence.

The use of crystals today is just as complex and exciting. Unfortunately, our scientists today will not admit that they are actually playing catch up with ancient civilizations. Rather they claimed to have discovered a new scientific breakthrough. This being said, there are great achievements in our time utilizing crystals. We incorporate crystals in our watches, in our computers as microprocessors, in our cell phones, communication lines and in LCD (Liquid Crystal Displays). The use of crystals goes far beyond modern technologies. Working with crystals every day, I know that they literally can change our physical, mental and spiritual lives.

Crystals are amazing! We know that when we hold a crystal in our hands and set an intention with our emotion and words that crystal will absorb, hold, empower and subsequently give out that intention. This is why healers, for thousands of years, have used crystals. We know now, that by taking a voltmeter and connecting the negative and positive wires to a crystal, you will get a voltage reading. We also know that by squeezing a crystal it will produce an electric current and when crystals are vibrating at a certain frequency, they can glow or even create extreme electricity. Crystals produce their own energy! There is so much more to be understood about crystals; we are just scratching the surface of the potential of these magical stones. Not only do we know that crystals can create their own energy, they also can hold information, energy and intentions. Knowing all of this, we begin to realize the almost limitless potential about what crystals can be used for in our lives.

One of the greatest examples of understanding the complex and magical powers of crystals is by studying our water; for water and crystals are forever intertwined. The element of Water does not just represent the life resource for plants and animals; it is also the carrier and container of information and energy. Very exciting research done by Dr. Emoto gives us a deeper understanding of the power of water and crystals in relationship to our feelings and intentions. Through his many amazing experiments, Dr. Masaru Emoto's work has confirmed that molecules of water are affected by thoughts, words and feelings. His work shows that water reacts to positive thoughts and words; water exposed to positive speech and thoughts would result in beautiful perfectly shaped crystals when that water was frozen; negative intentions would produce blobs of frozen crystal formations. His great work is a testament to humanity moving forward in understanding the complex and amazing brilliance of water. The element of Water within ourselves is just as vital to us as the oceans are to the living planet; every single particle of water, no matter how small, has a crystal structure within. Every droplet of water has the ability to absorb, contain, empower and then propel out our emotions, thoughts and feelings because of those tiny crystal structures! Once we understand that the human consciousness has an effect over water molecules, we can start healing our planet! We can start setting the right intentions for our environment and each other. Imagine for a moment the effect we have on every person and event; it is just like the effect of words and thoughts on the water crystals. All the food that we consume, the air that we breathe, the water that we drink and the people that we meet, have the element of water inside of them. Whether it is the fruits and vegetables or the animal products we are eating, there is water, and where there is water, there are crystals!

Knowing that crystals absorb our intentions, our emotions and our words, we must stop for a moment and ask ourselves: "What have I been saying and thinking about myself?" Just as Mother Earth's surface is 70% water, we too are made up of 70% water. By knowing that our thoughts and emotions have an effect over that water, we must be aware of what we are thinking and saying. I do not think it is any stretch of the imagination to say that our negative thoughts about Self outweigh the positive. Is your first thought when you get up in the morning and look into the mirror positive? We tend to concentrate on the negatives, don't we? We have a nasty habit of focusing on what we do not like about ourselves instead of seeing how wonderful we are as a perfect and glorious creation of Great Spirit and Mother Earth. Our egos and the worry of what others might think (which is also ego) keep us from truly loving ourselves, being kind to ourselves and remembering how perfect we really are.

When we think negatively about ourselves and only see that which we want to change, what do you think you are instilling into your crystals, into your water? The world is consumed with the image of beauty; of having the things that will make us beautiful or the title that will make us important. We have lost track of what beauty really is. We grow up in societies that teach us to concentrate on what is wrong with us, what we lack in life and then we wonder why we are sick all the time. What you believe about self, what you think about self, what words with which you choose to describe self, all are infused inside your crystals. In that way, we are making ourselves sick!

It is easy to see the effect polluted water has on our planet by looking at the massive livestock industries, fossil-fuel emissions and toxic runoffs. What about unhealthy water in ourselves? We cannot, as human beings, ever be disconnected from the four elements. What is true for Mother Earth is also true for us. Just as polluting Mother Earth's water harms our planet, so does polluting our water crystals with negative emotions, beliefs and thoughts. We can choose to believe every negative thing our parents, our teachers, our friends and family have taught us about Self. We can let that pollution run deeply into our veins and let it label us. We can either let those thoughts and words of others toxify our self-worth and ability to be the greatest we can be or we can choose to clean and clear our crystals and instill something better. As children, we absorb a lot and become defined by what adults tell us to believe, but as adults we have the choice! You have a choice in this very moment to believe what you want to believe about yourself.

Who are you? What do you love? What are your passions?

Why did you send yourself to this beautiful planet? What makes you laugh, smile, feel, love and be grateful? This is who you truly are! You are not the opinion of someone else! Remember this, remind yourself of it every day: do not succumb to the words or actions of others; be yourself. Instill in yourself, in your crystals who you really are and be proud of that. Hold your head up high and love your true self. Give your true self credit, honor and respect! Inside our water, our crystals, many of us still carry around the wounds and words of the past and let it rule our lives. If you do not wish for those old patterns and thoughts to rule your life then don't let them! Stop it! Just like that, stop it! The amazing thing about crystals is that they can be cleared and cleansed and asked to hold another intention. This is one of the most magical things about crystals. They can be reset. This is a true gift when it comes to those old wounds we have been carrying around for so long. You can let them go; you can move forward and not be so heavy with the negative thoughts you have trained yourself to carry.

What You Like or Dislike about Yourself

Having said that, the first thing I would like you to do is get yourself a pen and paper. I want you to take a moment and make a list of all the things you don't like about yourself. Really, put the book down. Before you read any further, get pen and paper and begin with the first list of all the things you dislike about yourself. Make it as long as you need it to be....

Now that your list is complete, I want to ask you: "Was it hard to come up with things you didn't like about yourself?" Probably not, right? It was pretty easy to write down several things; for many of us the list is not that short. Now, I want you to make another list, a list of things that you truly love about yourself, a list of all the things you honor and admire about you. Go ahead, make your list....

Was it more difficult? Is this list shorter than the first one? Did it take you more time to think about what you love about yourself? If so, don't beat yourself up, most of us have the same problem. It is a worldwide problem. We have been trained to see everything that is lacking, and then we are pushed to purchase something to make us feel better. We are taught to strive harder to achieve what is considered beautiful or prestigious enough to make us lovable or acceptable. Many of us do not step outside that *crazy box* often enough to realize it is all nonsense.

So with 'new' eyes, I want you to look over your first list of all the things you did not like about yourself; I want you to scratch off anything that has to do with what someone else might think of you or what someone wants you to be or become. If anything on the list has to do with what society thinks is beautiful or noteworthy, scratch it off. Anything left on the list will show you clearly what there still is to change and grow from. Much too often the things we do not like about ourselves, are the things or ideas that are instilled by someone else.

Guess what my friend? Only you can decide what is true for you; that should have nothing to do with what someone else might think of you. This is your life; you have chosen to come here. You are a beautiful individual, so make your life matter, make it count. You do not get yesterday back and life on this earth is short. Why waste your life, your health, your joy, and your opportunities here on this beautiful planet by installing your crystals full of negative thoughts and feelings? We must change the direction of our thoughts and emotions and not become so consumed with the negative. We were not born to this planet with negative beliefs about ourselves. As toddlers we didn't care how much we weighed or how many rolls we had around our waist. We didn't care what clothes we wore or what our hair looked like. All those thoughts and concerns were taught to us by a society ruled by ego. The only way back to love consciousness for all of us is if we can start loving and taking care of ourselves. We need to witness and value who we are as individuals and begin honoring ourselves for all that we are and all that we are not.

I urge you to become at peace with the journey you are on and who you are becoming. The best way to begin that path is by clearing and cleansing ourselves of the debris and the pollution we have been carrying in our water crystals. We can do that through our intention. Just as we can instill a crystal in our hands with the thoughts and emotions we wish it to hold, we can instill positive intentions inside of the crystals in our bodies, in our water. By using our gratitude, our love and positive energy, thoughts and emotions we can rewrite or override the negative we have stored inside our bodies since childhood.

The more we understand about the elements of Earth the more we understand about ourselves. We are not separate from Mother Earth, we ARE Mother Earth. Just like the planet, our bodies are amazing ecosystems. With only one in ten cells in our body being human we literally are walking ecosystems filled with microbes communicating chemically. Our bodies are the vessels in which all other elements live; they are the containers of unfathomable and complex systems, all working together. Our sense of self, our great I Am, our soul and our spirit are filled with the element of Fire, our passions. Our passions are what drive us forward. It is what helps propel us to do great things, discover and create just as our natural fires clear away the old and dead to new life. Our belief in Self resides in our water, in our crystals that then absorb, hold, empower and give life to that belief. Our wind is our voice that has the ability to communicate and inspire others, to move and plant the seeds of growth. If we cannot take care of and understand our planet, how can we understand and take care of ourselves and vice versa? We are forever intertwined and it is time to bring this great and most essential knowledge back to humanity. In many ways, we must look backwards to understand how we can go forward. Our indigenous cultures have known these sacred truths for thousands of years. Their knowledge is what will help heal us and help us continue on as a species, if only we will listen.

The Strongest of the Strong

As we listen to the words of our Indigenous Elders, our most revered men and women living today, our hearts must open and our ears must hear their truths. Through our ignorance and our egos we have found ourselves at a very serious crossroad. We are in a time in which none of us can deny the reality of global warming, and the impact humans have made towards this end. What we have done to the health of our planet it is profoundly and undeniably shocking. Humanity has ignored Mother Earth, the heart, the feminine, and love consciousness so severely that no one can deny, cover up or ignore the reality we find ourselves in today. We MUST start listening to our Elders! We must begin to cultivate a relationship with Mother Earth. We must once again place our utmost respect and protection on this life giving planet and each other. The time of greed must come to an end. The time of self-doubt, low self-esteem, the time of worrying about what others might think and the time of fitting in must stop if we are ever to make a difference. If we want the world to change WE must change it! We must take responsibility for the human activities that are negatively effecting this planet.

I cannot tell you how many times I have heard people make the comment: "Well, everything is ok because the aliens will fix it." Or: "Everything is the way it should be, Mother Earth will fix it." I am sorry, but this makes my passion turn into flames! Let us just think for a moment. If there was a wise elderly woman making a beautiful vegetable garden, with herbs and medicinal plant in which she can feed and sustain herself and her community; then this garden is destroyed by a bunch of teenagers playing soccer. Are we expected to believe that she needs to regrow that garden and give the food to the kids that knowingly destroyed it? Or do we think that someone else will simply appear and give the garden back? No, of course not! We know better! We know that we are hurting our planet just like those teenagers knew not to play soccer in the garden; yet many believe it is ok to do whatever they want to do and take no responsibility for their actions.

There is an old truth that states: "The more you know, the more you are responsible for!" We DO know better than to pollute our drinking water; we know better than to clear-cut the forest that gives us oxygen and is home to countless species; we know better than to trawl our oceans until there are no fish left, yet we keep on doing it. We are responsible for the mess; therefore, we must be responsible in cleaning it up! We are not allowed to take everything and give nothing back. We as human beings are not allowed to produce whatever trash we like and just bury it or dump it in the oceans. We are not allowed to do this, it is against the circle of life and it is creating a great chasm in the natural process of things.

It is our responsibly to stop our supreme way of thinking about ourselves as the rulers over all other species. In fact, we are the only species that creates trash, the only ones that take more than we need and the only ones destroying the ecosystems. We have to stop, we have to come to the understanding that money and greed will only lead to our detriment. Ego has ruled far too long and has destroyed far too much. It is up to us, the human being, to turn it around. We caused the problem, and we are responsible for fixing the problem (Not aliens from another planet!). Just as parents doing their children's homework does not teach the child responsibility or their school lesson, extraterrestrials fixing our problems will not teach us how to solve our own mess!

So no, I do not believe we can do whatever we want, use whatever we want, trash what we want, destroy what we want and someone else will just appear out of the heavens and make it all better. We have to take responsibility, and we must start listening to our indigenous cultures who have been teaching the truth the whole time; who have been warning us against the effects of our own ignorance. It is time for us to make a stand and become the strongest of the strong. It is time for us to stand resolute in the shift we wish to create. It is time for us to be: "The ones we have been waiting for." It is time for us to stand together and make the greatest unified voice ever heard, shouting: "We love each other; we love ourselves; we love this planet and we love all other living species, and we are willing to change our ways of being." Let us stand together and shout: "I value love more than ego!" It is time to make the change, brothers and sisters. No one else is coming to clean up our mess; we must do it ourselves.

I believe that we truly are the strongest of the strong; we are those we have been waiting for, just as the Elders have been telling us. It is time for us to be strong, unified and unwavering in the one thing that will change the world we live in. It is time to live from LOVE.

We have to understand that each of us matter, that we are all different and on different paths and taking different journeys and that in our differences we are great. We must learn to love ourselves for the passions that we have, the voices that we can use to put those passions into motion. It is time to be grateful for this perfect body Mother Earth has given us and for the water inside of us that holds our powerful beliefs and core essence of what we can create. We must understand our Water element and the power it holds within each of us. We often think that what we believe or what we feel as an individual does not carry much weight. Let me tell you: a drop of water continually dripping can erode a mountain! Water can dissolve more substances than any other liquid, including sulfuric acid! Believing in yourself and what you stand for can create huge changes! When single droplets of water come together it can wash entire buildings off of their foundations, throw entire cargo ships up and onto the shore and erode away rocks creating massive canyons. Just as a mighty river begins as single droplets of water melting away from the snow high on a mountain peak, we too have this power inside of us. We can come together with one passion, one goal and one great dream, to heal our hearts and our home.

Water, truly, is the most important resource on our planet and for all the life out here. The water inside us is like the water on our planet. It can be polluted, stagnated and unclean, or it can be crystal clear, pure and life giving. Our water crystals can be changed by positive and negative, good and bad. It is the keeper of our negative and positive energies, our emotions, our thoughts and words. So let us be very aware of what we are doing to the water in our bodies as well as to the water of our planet. Knowing that the water on our planet and in our bodies contain crystalline structures inside, we start to realize the incredible importance of keeping our liquid crystals unpolluted.

Our solid crystals, on the other hand, are unchanging, powerful pure living energy machines. I believe the use of crystals is the very key to repairing the damage we have done, not only to our bodies but also to the planet itself. How can we use crystals to heal ourselves and heal our planet? Well, the solution is actually quite simple. There are four important things when talking about crystals. One, all things in our universe are made up of energy, including every thought, emotion, belief and word we have ever had in our lifetime. Two, as I have said before, the strongest energy always wins. Three, love is the strongest vibrational energy on earth. Four, crystals can absorb, hold, amplify and then present what information you program them to hold. Realizing this, we have the formula to change our world for the better.

We begin to see that once again Mother Earth has given us freely the answers and the tools we need to heal ourselves and to clean the mess we have made, here on our planetary home. When it comes to crystals there is so much for us to learn whether it be scientific, metaphysical, spiritual or philosophical. In our culture today we all have seen crystals in nature, in jewelry shops, as beautiful little decorative pieces but they are so much more. Crystals come in every shape size and color and each crystal has its own unique specialty in terms of its healing abilities. Instead of going into all these specific abilities, it is of utmost importance now to know and utilize the overall purpose and power of the whole. The most important thing to know about crystals is that they hold and give off energy, frequency and vibration.

The same three things Nikola Tesla said were the secrets to understanding the universe! He did recognize that everything in the universe, including you and me, are pure forms of energy, vibrating at different levels of frequency. Crystals are special because their molecules and atoms are structured in very precise geometric patterns, and they emit the highest vibrational frequencies of any solid atom that we have on earth. The most amazing thing to me is that by holding them in our hands, we can utilize them in such a way that their vibrational frequency interacts with ours. How incredible is it that these beautiful crystals not only hold patterns of sacred geometry within their atomic structures, but that they also can interact with us, change our frequency and help us manifest what our heart's intentions are? They are also constantly interacting with each other! Each crystal holds a specific and unique frequency just like we do; there is one difference, they are completely and forever in tune with and in sync with each other.

Crystals hold and emanate their pure and unchanged frequency constantly without waver; they are not like us in the sense that we have up and down emotions, thoughts and patterns. This is why crystals have such an impact on the human being. Simply by holding crystals in our hands or wearing a crystal around our necks, we reap the benefits of their pure high vibrational frequency. This in itself is one of the greatest gifts Mother Earth has given us. It gets even better. When we hold a crystal in our hands and feel our good intentions, affirmations and prayers, these crystals will hold, make stronger and give out those very same things with the highest and purest energy. We are not like crystals; we do not have a constant high and unwavering pure frequency. We have good days and bad days; we have negative and positive thoughts, feelings and emotions. We also have our egos playing a role in how our energy is vibrating and deal with duality all the time. Therefore, it is so important for us to utilize these beautiful gifts to help us maintain a higher frequency. Using crystals is not a new-age phenomenon; it is not just a concept or a hip, cool thing that is all the rage in the spiritual community. They are truly powerful vibrating frequency machines that can and do affect our energy physically, mentally, spiritually and even atomically.

How to Program Your Crystals

A frequently asked question is: "How do I program my crystals?" First, there is no one set of words that can do it. Remember it is your intention, your emotion and affirmations that set the intentions into your crystals; not a set of memorized words! Memorized words are simply a set of words someone else made up and that you remember; they have nothing to do with your true emotions and pure intentions. The only rule to setting your intentions into your crystals is that you must feel them, not just think them. A thought does not carry the power or energy as high as your emotions and feelings do. Remember, love is the strongest energy in the world and the fastest way to get your love energy the highest is by feeling gratitude. Before holding a crystal in your hand and programming it, take just a moment to think about something you are grateful for. Let this feeling rise as high and as profoundly as possible. Now you are ready to install the prayers, affirmations, and wishes into the crystal.

By holding the crystal in your hands (remember the feet is where the body takes in energy and the hands are where energy is given out) and feeling the intentions, your crystal will start to absorb, contain, make stronger and emanate out the frequency of what you have programmed it to do. One important thing in programming your crystal is the kind of intention you put in the crystal. Let us take, for example, someone who wants to bring a partner into his life. He should not hold in his hands a crystal and feel the loneliness, the unhappiness and dissatisfaction of not having that lover. He should feel the gratitude and the excitement and the love he feels to have a new partner coming to him. The same goes for a person installing a crystal with healing for the waters of Mother Earth; he should not hold a crystal in his hands and think of all the pollution, stagnation, and species die off in the ocean; he should concentrate his emotions on a healthy ocean full of protected happy species unharmed by radiation and pollution.

Remember to put in the crystal the positive you want to see and do not feel and feed the negative. Another question about crystals I receive a lot is: "If I am having a bad day, and I feel negative thoughts and emotions, will my crystal absorb that negativity?" The answer is simply: "No." Remember, our solid crystals are pure vibrating frequency and energy, and the strongest energy always wins. This is simply how all energy works. If Mother Earth's physical crystals are of the highest and purest energy, they simply cannot absorb negativity. The high frequency and vibration always overpowers the negative.

So if you are having a bad day, and you feel down or irritated or even angry, this is when you need the help of your crystal the most! For example, we had a study done in Japan, on the effect of a crystal installed with love and protection for radiated water. Radiated water from the Fukushima radiation spill was hooked up to computers by a team of scientists to monitor the effects of this love infused crystal on the radiated water molecules. Within two minutes of the crystal being dropped into the water, the radiation was undetectable. Indeed! Undetectable! Nothing was done to the water except for placing a crystal inside, that was installed with love, gratitude and the protection of our oceans. The crystal did not then contain any radiation. It did not absorb the negative radiation but instead deleted it. Again, the strongest energy always wins. Radiation is just an energy, but the intention of love, gratitude and a healed and healthy ocean was far more powerful. Our crystals cannot absorb our negative emotions and thoughts; they always contain the highest energy.

Which brings us to our next question that is always asked: "When or how often should I clean and clear my crystals?" Many people are constantly clearing their crystals but there is no need to do so. There are only two reasons why you should ever clear and clean your crystals. When you receive a crystal from someone, or you buy a crystal and you do not know what has been installed in that crystal already, it is a good reason to clean and clear that crystal. When you get a new crystal for yourself, I would suggest clearing it so that you can then install what you need it for. Secondly, if you have a crystal you do healing with, it is good to clear it before using it for another healing session. For example, if a client came to my home for a personal session and was suffering from a particular health issue, I would take a cleared crystal and I would ask the crystal to use all of its energy for the purpose of helping with this particular problem. If the client would have breast cancer, I would ask the crystal to help use all of its energy for the breaking apart and deletion of cancer. The next day I have a client with migraines. I would not use the same crystal without clearing and cleaning it. I would first need to clear that crystal and then install the intention for the crystal to use all of its energy to help this person with his headaches. The key here is that you are asking a healing crystal to use all of its energy, its frequency and vibration to help with one specific problem. Crystals can contain and hold as much information as you wish to give it. A crystal can never get full; this is why just a fraction of quartz crystal is needed to run the largest man made computers in the world. Their storage space for information, energy and abilities is limitless. But if you want your crystal to use all of its energy for one specific problem then you will need to clear it before using it for another issue. For our personal crystals that we wear around our neck or keep with us in our pockets; they can never be filled up. You can just keep asking the crystal to hold more and more intentions and prayers to help you throughout your life.

The question that is always asked is: "How do I clear and clean my crystals?" There are a lot of ideas out there of how to clear crystals. I have heard everything from salt water and sunlight to even fire, none of which are good ideas. In fact, you are most likely to harm your crystal than anything else. If you leave your crystals in sunlight, perhaps over a long period of time, the crystal will start to clear itself, but it is not likely. Sunlight can also damage the color of certain crystals. It will not hurt the function of a crystal, but it can damage the look. Fire is the worst idea I have ever heard. This will without a doubt harm your crystal and should never be done. Salt water will not clear your crystal at all and in fact, some crystals like Selenite will dissolve in salt water. Unless you are giving it away to the ocean, you should never put a crystal in salt water for clearing purposes. By putting any crystal in water, fresh or salty, all you have done is blessed the water crystals with your crystal, not clear it. The best and most effective way to clear any kind of crystal is by using moonlight. Moonlight clears and cleanses your crystal in the most effective and gentle way. You can set your crystals outside overnight (as long as it is not new moon and there is no light emanating off the moon) and your crystals will be cleared and cleansed. You can also set your crystals in a windowsill inside your home for the same effect. Remember you do not have to be able to see the moonlight to clear your crystal. It can be raining or snowing or cloudy; the energy of the moon will still do its job. In order for this to work you must set the intention that you want your crystals to be cleared, hold them in your hands and ask them to be cleared by the moon. Wearing your personal crystal around your neck and going for a walk in the moonlight will not clear your crystal. It can only be done with the intention to clear it.

Giving Your Crystals Back to Mother Earth

Many of you have heard me say: "It is time for us to give our crystals back to Mother Earth's wild waters." It is not because Mother Earth is selfish, and she wants them back. It is because every particle of water has a crystal structure inside, no matter how large or small that water is, no matter if that water comes from a mud puddle or a raindrop, your fruits or vegetables, the saliva in your mouth or from the ocean. And...crystals speak to each other! Dr. Emoto (in my opinion, one of the greatest men to ever exist in our time) showed the world how our words and intentions influence the crystalline structures in water. He showed us that by speaking the words "hate," "violence," "rape," or "murder" changes that crystal structure into something resembling a brownish yellow blob. The words like "love," "kindness" and "compassion" changed that same crystal structure into something resembling a bright and shining snowflake.

Many experiments have been done to show that our words have an influence over our water crystals. This is why, for instance, praying for a plant actually makes that plant grow stronger, healthier and more vibrant versus yelling and using hateful words at a plant, deforms and kills it. This is the very reason why many indigenous cultures teach us to place the seeds we are about to plant in our gardens in our mouth before planting them. The seeds in your mouth get to know your DNA, what vitamins you lack en what nutrients you need from that plant. By placing the seeds in your mouth before you plant them; you can give your prayers, gratitude and blessings. We know that our words are powerful, and our emotions are even more potent and those words and emotions affect the seeds. Knowing that every particle of water on our planet contains a crystal and knowing that all crystals can absorb, hold, make stronger, then emanate out our intentions, we can start healing our planet.

Now, when we are ready to give crystals back to Mother Earth's waters, we hold a solid crystal in our hands and set our intentions and our prayers inside of it. We throw that crystal into the water, and our prayers are then shared to all the other particles of crystals in that body of water. It goes even beyond that body of water, because water does something amazing, it evaporates! No matter how small the water particle is, it still holds information. That evaporated water travels up into the air containing your prayers, and it will share your prayers to all the other particles of water in the air. Then those particles gather themselves into clouds where again your intentions, and the energy of your prayers are shared to all the moisture in that cloud. As the cloud gets heavier and heavier, it begins to rain. All of those little raindrops containing and sharing your prayers fall back down to the earth where they land on our crops, our plants and animals, back to the land and waters of our beautiful blue planet where they will continue to recycle themselves.

Your one prayer in one crystal can help heal our planet and all that inhabit Her. It is truly time for us to give our crystals back to Mother Earth. Fill these crystals with your prayers and your intentions for clean, clear waters, healthy happy animals and a higher and more loving frequency on our planet. So many of us have crystals in our homes, but how many of us can honestly say, all of those crystals are being used? Most of the time they are put on a shelf, because they look pretty. Consider, these crystals can be used for a much greater purpose! All crystals can be programmed, and all crystals should go back to our beautiful Mother, if they are not a working crystal. What I mean by that is, if you have crystals at home that you are using for healing work either for yourself or others, or it is your personal crystal that you wear, continue to work with this crystal—it has a job. For those crystals that are decorative, give them a job; put them to work by placing your prayers inside them and give them back to the wild water. Give them back to Mother Earth in our lakes, streams, rivers, ponds and oceans where they can create the greatest good. Many of us place them in nature where they can give their energy to a tree or a small patch of ground where the moisture connects them together, and this is also powerful. However, by placing the crystal in wild water your prayers can reach a far greater distance!

No matter where I travel on this beautiful planet, I take crystals with me. I do not take big, expensive, rare crystals; but simple quartz crystals. Quartz crystal is the most abundant, easy to find, least aggressive to obtain from our beloved earth and quite simply the most powerful crystal to use. There are many, many different kinds of crystals out there and they all have their special gifts to give. Take, for example, rose quarts; it can be used for opening the heart chakra. Labradorite, often employed by shamans, is used for gaining knowledge and guidance. Black tourmaline is used for protection, grounding and healing. Each and every crystal has its own special gift to give, but to be honest clear quartz can do the job of all of them. It is inexpensive and readily available and can be found at the surface of the earth.

Another question I often receive is: "Would you like to meet my personal crystal skull?" Many people who have crystals cut into a human skull form have names for them. They even treat them differently from their regular crystals. To be very blunt, no matter what form a crystal is cut into, whether it be a heart, a pyramid or a skull, it is the same crystal! Just because a crystal cutter has cut and polished a crystal into a skull form does not make it a being with a name! There are 12 crystal skulls on this planet (we are waiting for the 13th) that are not from planet Earth. It is said when mankind moves into love consciousness, the 13th crystal skull will be gifted to our planet. When they are finally all together their information will be granted to mankind. For now, humanity is still living in ego consciousness, and we have not been able to access or be gifted with this information.

Several of the ancient and very special crystal skulls we have, are tested and studied by many scientists from around the world. They have unexplainable abilities, anomalies and are proven not to be from Earth. The skulls are believed to contain the information of its source and of the beings living on that planet and other important knowledge. All crystals that are from planet Earth, no matter what kind, shape or size, are still 'just' Earth crystals. Cutting and polishing a crystal into a skull does not make it any different than if it were in a raw form.

When we take a good look at our present situation on our planet, whether it be the devastation of forests, the depletion of animal species, the polluting of our waters or the global warming crisis, one thing is for sure: We have to do something! We are the strongest of the strong for a reason. We are the ones living in the here and now, and we have to make a change. Our planet simply cannot keep sustaining humanity the way we are living; it is an impossibility. We must find our way back to our higher Selves and the reason why we chose to come to this planet in the first place. We must break free from those boxes that have kept us mentally and emotionally trapped. We have to start standing for what we as precious individuals believe in. We have to break free from the chains of fear, that old pattern of mental illness that cripples so many. We must overcome the constant trap of what others might think of us; we can make our brave stand on loving ourselves, loving this planet and loving others. When we find our power back we stop instilling those hateful words and thoughts about ourselves inside of our water crystals. We will stop giving our energy to the unnecessary and begin using our energy for the good. We can start focusing on what we can do instead of what we lack. The truth is we have all we need to make the difference; we just need to get to work. We have crystals and by placing our prayers in them and giving them back to the water, these prayers can start influencing the water crystals and make the world a better place.

Creating Your Sacred Circle or Medicine Wheel: Water

The Water element is the source of all life. It is the most precious and valuable element on our planet and to all that call Her home. Knowing the critical state our water is in on our planet today we can see the great need for our waters to be healed. And so with all of our respect, love and honor for our Water element within our own bodies and on the body of the Great Mother we are ready to complete our medicine wheel.

I now ask you to choose a crystal to represent the direction of the North, the keeper of water and ice and the color of white. After taking off your shoes and doing the breathing meditation and awakening your senses, enter your circle and face the direction of the North, in front of the area in which you will place the stone to connect the circle. While holding the crystal in your hands and closing your eyes, you begin to feel all the gratitude for every drink of water you have ever been given, every meal you have ever eaten, for every living thing that has provided you with the clothes you wear to the wood that creates your home. Be grateful for all living creatures that water has sustained and given life to.

Let your mind envision the great icecaps of our planet and send your love, blessings and gratitude for the enormous role they play in cooling our planet. Visualize all the life that lives within our oceans, our rivers, lakes and streams from the smallest plankton to the largest whales and be grateful! Feel the love you have for this blue planet of ours and the countless particles of water circulating our globe that contain crystals within them.

Offer your gratitude for the Elders of the North, the Saami, Inuit, Nenets, and Chukchi who hold the knowledge and great wisdom of the element Water. Take the time to be grateful for the water inside of you, for the crystals that can hold your thoughts and emotions, your prayers and wishes and remember once again that you are not separate from beautiful Mother Earth but you are a part of Her.

Be grateful to be a human being and love yourself, your gifts, and your ability to be a great transformer on this planet for the better. Allow yourself to awaken to the knowledge that you are able to heal yourself with your thoughts and prayers, your words and emotions. Because your crystals will always absorb, contain, make stronger and then give out what you put in them. Say your own individual prayers for yourself and for your beloved Mother Earths' waters to heal. When your prayers are finished, you can place the crystal into the circle facing the direction of the North.

How to Use Your Sacred Circle or Medicine Wheel

You now have completed the circle of the four directions and should understand what each color, direction and element represent. Understanding the four directions and their corresponding elements is very important. As I said earlier, the Earth is not just a random rock orbiting through space; she is a Sacred Being, the Great Mother to us all and the heart chakra of our universe. Our beautiful Mother Earth is 4.45 billion years old and has fed, sheltered, cared for and embraced many different living species from the first single-celled organisms, to the fish and amphibians, the dinosaurs, birds, mammals and eventually we, the human being. She has been the caretaker of everyone and everything that has ever lived an Earth life. She has provided us with the food we eat and the water we drink. She has freely given every shelter, every fire and of course every breath of oxygen in our lungs. We need Her; we need Her for our very survival, but She does not need us! We forget this fact in our ignorance and in our flamboyant egotistical ways of living.

We are not the greatest creation on Earth; the Earth is the greatest creation! She has seen species come and go, and yet, She remains. Around 200,000 years ago we, the human being arrived and in that time She has watched us succeed and She has watched us fail. Yet, no matter what we have done, She has given us life continuously and selflessly. Mother Earth has been here for eons, and She will continue to exist but the fate of humanity is in our own hands. We must learn that our actions upon this great planet will determine how long we will be here. In order to start living in harmony with Mother Nature, we must, once again, see ourselves as part of the Great Circle of Life. One way to rekindle that knowing inside of ourselves is by taking the time to honor the four directions and elements that bring Mother Earth and Her children together.

When we create a Sacred Circle to represent the four directions and the four elements, we must do it with understanding, compassion and gratitude for the elements on the planet and within ourselves. Once the Medicine Wheel or Sacred Circle has been completed you are ready to use it for your prayers and meditations, and as a constant reminder to Self that you are connected, important and have a purpose!

Remember, before you begin your prayers and offerings at your newly created Sacred Circle, you should let the worries of the day go, clear your head and become reverent.

I always begin my prayers facing the direction towards the North and then move "sunwise" or clock wise around the Sacred Medicine Wheel. You can start your prayers where *you* would like to begin of course, but always move "sunwise" around your circle, stopping at each direction to honor the corresponding element of Mother Earth, ending each prayer by giving a small offering to fill in the Medicine Wheel circle. For example, I place flowers, seeds and leaves between the stone representing the South towards the stone symbolizing Earth in the West. From the stone representing Earth towards the Crystal in place of the North, I lay branches, stones or anything else that represents the Earth element. From the North crystal towards the stone representing the East for Fire, I place crystals to symbolize my gratitude for the water. From the stone in the East towards the South, I place lava rock or things that represent my gratitude and prayers for Fire, my passions and purpose.

Remember, there is no one right or wrong offering. Your offerings and gifts that will complete the circle should be directly from your heart. An offering can be anything natural that you wish to give as a thank you to the Mother. Do not forget to offer tobacco or sage if you have it. Many times the smoke of the tobacco is used to offer prayers. For one, the tobacco itself represents the *earth* element that we love and respect. Secondly, we use *fire* to light the tobacco, representing not only the respect for the east and the sun that gives us life but also honoring the fire from within. By lighting the tobacco on fire we are reminded of our prayers and passions that live within us. Thirdly, we use our breath, our *wind*, the mover of seeds to bring the smoke into our mouths where it is then connected to our saliva, our *water* and the keeper of our knowledge, wisdom, prayers. That smoke is then blown out towards heaven and earth and all that is in-between sharing our prayers and emotions through our wind.

North – White – Water

Now that you have completed the task of creating your Sacred Circle it is ready for you to use. Begin by standing inside the circle in front of the crystal you have chosen to represent the North. Close your eyes and feel your presence of body and soul on this beautiful planet. Feel your feet on the earth and the moisture that is available, making it possible for all sorts of plants and fungi to grow and create our living flora and fauna. Breathe in the moisture of the air and feel gratitude for the rain storms that bless us each season. Take a moment to appreciate the great ice sheets at our poles that balance the temperature on our beautiful planet. Be aware of your precious body that is made up of 70% water. Take a moment to feel the gratitude you have for this amazing and miraculous blue planet, and then begin your prayers.

Start by giving your gratitude for the color white and the element of water. Feel the honor and respect for the Elders, the wise men and women who have kept their traditions and teachings of wisdom alive on our planet. Give thanks for the water on our planet and ask a blessing for the waters to be healed, to be clean and full of life. Ask a blessing for the waters inside of yourself to also be healed, as well as for each of us to remember to live from love, kindness and purity of heart. Take a moment to remember that your crystals contain the highest vibrations of gratitude and self-awareness in all that you do.

Take as much time as you need to express yourself and connect with the Water element. When you are finished, offer a small gift to the North. This can be done in many ways, such as placing dried sage, tobacco, flowers, corn, cotton or whatever you might feel is appropriate. You can also offer the smoke from tobacco by blowing the smoke towards the direction of the North.

When your prayer to the North is complete, you turn and face the direction of the East.

East – Red – Fire

Once you have offered your prayers to the direction of the North, move so that you are standing inside the circle facing the direction of the East and the stone or crystal you have placed there. Feel your bare feet in the soil and the sunlight on your skin, feel your heart beating in your chest and let the gratitude for your life and your purpose begin to surface. Facing the direction of the East you offer your great thanks for the sun that rises each new day giving you a new opportunity to be the greatest I AM that you can be. Feel appreciation for the warmth and the life that the sun provides for our beautiful Mother Earth and all of her creatures great and small.

Feel honor and respect for the Elders, the grandmothers and grandfathers who come from the East, for all their wisdom and knowledge that is still being taught to those who will listen. Ask a blessing upon the indigenous cultures from the East to be protected, honored and cared for and a blessing upon ourselves that we may always remember the fire that burns within each of us. May you always remember your passions so that you can live with a burning purpose upon this planet; that you may burn away those things which are dead and suffocating your fires ability to burn brightly. Take a moment to offer your gratitude to the East, the color of red and the keeper of the element Fire.

When your prayers are finished, you kneel down and offer a gift or send your prayers into the air with the tobacco. Then move inside the circle to face the direction of the South.

South – Yellow – Wind

Once you are facing the direction of the South close your eyes and feel the air moving across your skin and through your hair. Smell the air with its subtle hints of soil, the many plants and flowers, trees and pollens. When you feel you are connected to the direction of the South and the element of Wind, begin your prayer. Present your gratitude for the direction of the South, the color of yellow and the keeper of the element Wind. Be thankful for all the many varieties of plant life and vegetation, for the fruits and vegetables, our nuts and flowers. Ask a blessing upon the great rain forests in the South and all those who inhabit them, that they may be watched over and protected. Offer your most humble respect for the indigenous peoples, the true guardians of our Sacred Mother, who live within these forests and pray for their safety at this time.

Be grateful for the Elders, the grandmothers and grandfathers, the men and women, the children, the forests and animals in the South and pray that all of humanity will wake up and safeguard their future. Feel appreciation for the powerful wind you carry inside yourself and ask a blessing that you may find the courage to speak your truth at all times and to use your words for creating positivity. May the power of your voice be used to give breath to your purpose and passion, to lift others up and fertilize each other's goodness. Let us remember to never use our wind to erode away another brother's or sister's potential but always give oxygen to their fires within to grow and burn bright. May your voice find the courage and the power to help humankind heal from their old wounds and worries.

Take a few moments to say your own personal prayers.

Kneel down when you are finished and offer a small gift to the stone then blow your tobacco smoke into the direction of the South. Now turn so that you are facing the direction of the West.

West – Black – Earth

Please stand on the inside of the circle facing the stone or crystal you have placed there to represent the direction of the West, the color of black and the element of Earth. Close your eyes and feel all the gratitude of love you have for the soil that provides us with all the beauty and resources that is given to each of us every day. Give acknowledgment to the great forests, mountains, jungles, deserts, grasslands and all the animals and plants that make our planet so beautiful and diverse. Pray to the direction of the West and give your unwavering gratitude for the Elders, the grandmothers and grandfathers and the wise ones that come from the West. Be grateful for all those who have come before you, every culture and tribe, every color of brother and sister who has shared this great planet with you. Feel appreciation for your body that this Earth has sustained from the first day you arrived here until this day. Ask a blessing upon yourself and for your brothers and sisters that we all might remember our own value and bigger purpose as the children of Mother Earth. Offer thanks for the time of blackness, the time of silence, meditation and listening.

Take a moment to ask for what blessings you stand in need of, then offer your prayers of gratitude and love for all that the Earth has provided you with, then kneel down and offer your gift to the West.

The Center of the Circle, Great Spirit

Once you are finished offering your prayers and gratitude for the four directions and their corresponding elements, it is time to stand in the center of your Sacred Circle and lift your head to the heavens. With your arms outstretched offer your prayers to Great Spirit, the source of all life. Feel your most heartfelt love and appreciation for the creator and for your own Great I Am that chose to come to this planet and take this amazing journey. Feel appreciation for your human connections of family and friends and the ability to take part in being a human being on this magnificent planet. Be grateful for all of your life experiences no matter how challenging they have been. For they have helped you learn and grow to become the person you are today. Each life lesson has taught you to become better, stronger and wiser throughout your journey. Pray that you may always feel the connection to Source and be reminded of how great you are as an individual who is helping to create human consciousness here on Earth. May you at all times walk with honor, respect, humility and love in your heart. Take as much time as you wish to offer your prayers and ask for those blessings you stand in need of at this time. Finish, by blowing your prayers into the air above you, either by the tobacco smoke or simply your breath.

Bowing to the Sacred Mother

Finally in closing, kneel down and by placing your hands on the beloved Mother bowing your head in reverence, begin your prayers to your Mother Earth. Remember that the only way to say a prayer perfectly is if it comes directly from your own heart. Speak to your Mother, the giver of your life, your body, every wonderful breath of air, the source of every meal, every drink of water, the mother to all living creatures and the beauty of this world. She is the Great Goddess, the Divine Feminine, the Mother to all our ancestors and those yet to come. Thank the Mother for the gift of being a human being, since it is a true honor and a great privilege. Thank Her for the green grasses, the blue waters, the creatures great and small, the herbs and medicines She provides for us all and for the bounty and beauty She selflessly and continually gives.

Feel gratitude for the swimmers, the crawlers, the flyers, the four legged, the two legged and the one legged, our Grand Elders, the trees and for the fruits, vegetables, grains and nuts that sustain your life. Speak to your beloved Mother and know that She hears your words. Offer Her gratitude, honor and respect. Pray for not only yourself but for all of humanity to remember Her as a living being. As you kneel down, with your hands on the earth and your head bowed, send Her love, tell Her how much you love Her and grow your connection to Her strong again. Take the time to speak your own words to your Sacred Mother, let the depths of your heart pour out and share your emotions with Her. Offer your prayers and your blessings; then when you are finished, offer the smoke of the tobacco or what gift you have to give to the center of the circle. With your prayers now complete you can step out of the circle.

The Sacred Circle you have created has been completed with your heart and soul. Your words and your emotions have made it sacred and you can revisit this circle anytime you wish to offer prayers or ask for something that you need. Let it be a place of remembrance of the four elements that forever connect you to the Great Mother. Each time you stand at the stones, remember the blessings of the elements within yourself. This is a place that is yours, a place that you can turn to day and night to offer your respect, honor, love and appreciation for all that exists on this planet. This Sacred Circle is a place where you can pray for the things you stand in need of. It is a place that is reverent, a place in which you can deeply connect to your beloved Mother; a place where you can begin growing a strong and deeper personal relationship with Her. This is your Sacred Site! We might forget Her from time to time; we might forget that we are forever connected to Her through the very same energy that runs through our bodies, to the wind, the water, the soil and the fire, but She has not forgotten. She is always there, always listening and always teaching; we simply have to remember to go back home and be present to Her.

Part II

Ancient Sacred Crystals
around the World

Ancient Sacred Crystals

As many of you know, one of my jobs as Little Grandmother has been to place nine very Sacred and incredibly powerful Crystals into high vibrating locations around the world. These locations have to do with the telluric lines, electrical currents or leylines that intersect or cross over one another, producing a high conducting electrical current. Many times you can find ancient places of worship, pyramids or stone circles in these geomagnetic fields. It is a misconception that these locations on our planet are sacred because of a building, a pyramid, stone circles or a church. Our ancient ancestors knew where the telluric lines intersected and constructed their places of worship on these high vibrational places. When I became Little Grandmother, I was gifted with nine precious and Sacred Crystals. Seven of these Crystals were to be placed in very precise locations on the globe where these telluric lines intersect to help heal and strengthen our Mother Earth's energy field. The other two Crystals were to be used for specific ceremonies, one for the awakening of the Sacred Feminine on 10-10-10 in Arkansas USA which I talk about in my first book, "Message for the Tribe of Many Colors." The other was to be used for the healing of Mother Earth and Her children at a specific point and time. (That crystal went to Japan to heal the wounds caused by the Fukushima radiation meltdown, discussed later in the book.)

In my first book: "Message for the Tribe of Many Colors," I share the stories of placing the first four Crystals into the Earth in depth. Here I will give a quick overview of those ceremonies and their locations.

Arkansas

Using one of the two "specially destined" crystals I was given the amazing opportunity and humbling experience of conducting a ceremony for the healing of the Sacred Feminine. This ceremony took place in the Northwest Central part of Arkansas. This is a magical and very special place filled with many underground crystal caves and rivers. The moment your feet touch the soil one cannot help but realize there is something so very special taking place. The earth itself almost vibrates, and it is no wonder: this area has one of the highest crystal concentrations in the world! On a beautiful morning at exactly 10:10am on 10/10/10, we began our ceremony. This ceremony was held for the sole purpose of bringing the return of the Sacred Feminine energy back to our planet. I remember my Elder Eesawuu from the Hopi tribe saying it was the day that the Great Feminine took Her rightful place upon Her throne. There were many ceremonies that day. Some ceremonies took place on top of the highest mountain peaks and ice shelves in the North where they "lit the fires atop the world." In these great ceremonies the male Elders paid their respect and gave the authority over to the female Elders. I still carry a small bundle of ash from these sacred fires that was gifted to me weeks after the ceremony was conducted. Having taken part in such a pivotal moment in time left a great sense of awe and reverence for Mother Earth and for the feminine deep inside my soul.

Since the day of the ceremony held in the beautiful nature of Arkansas, over 500 earthquakes have been reported from the crystal activation area. The Great Feminine has awoken!

Santa Fe

The first of the Sacred seven Crystals went into the Native American lands near Santa Fe New Mexico during the ceremony: "The Return of the Ancestors," in 2009. This Crystal went into the Earth together with all our prayers and gratitude for those who came before us, with respect and honor for our ancestors, the wisdom they carried and for the healing of the wounded masculine and feminine within humanity. This was, to this day, the most intense and hardest ceremony I have ever been a part of. I have never witnessed so many spirits and ancestors willing to be present and seen while taking an active part in such a difficult healing ceremony. As we prayed to let go of our wounds as men and women and to forgive the unimaginable suffering, expectations, and faults of each other, I will always remember the strength of my Elders Eesawuu and Sister Wolf who were there to guide me and give me strength.

Redwoods

The second crystal was given to the great Redwood trees on the coast of California. Our ancient trees are considered to be the "Grand Elders" of our beautiful planet. Some trees like the Bristle Cone pine from California's White Mountains live to be almost 5,000 years old! I have truly loved trees my entire life and spent many, many hours playing and sleeping in their branches. Trees bring me a sense of gratitude and even nostalgia, as some of my favorite memories as a child are in and amongst the trees. From being a little girl climbing in my great grandma Jensen's apple tree and sleeping in its branches, to my grove of cotton wood trees down by the river that became my home, I have always felt a great love for trees. I have been granted great opportunities to see some of the most sacred trees on the planet, from the precious Red Cypress of Taiwan, the revered Japanese Cedar, the honored White Ghost Gum trees in Australia to the Beloved Yew trees in Britain, Scotland and Wales. No matter where I go, I can find the Grand Elders standing tall in all their brilliant glory.

Trees have been a sacred focal point for many indigenous cultures, not only for their practical value for food, medicines, shelter and fuel but often also for spirituality, worship and celebration. The significance of trees to our beautiful planet and all that inhabit her is truly immeasurable. Our ancient trees, including the redwoods, are living beings that have seen countless generations come and go. They hold a great deal of memory, wisdom and knowledge. Like giant keepers of information, they invoke a feeling of awe and wonderment. I can personally attest to this feeling while standing among the redwoods which can grow up to 379 feet or 115 meters tall! The crystal was given to the Redwood trees, the Grand Elders with great respect, honor and prayers for humanity to open their hearts to the Natural world again.

Hawaii

The third of the Sacred Crystals was given to the sacred lands of the Hawaiian Island Maui in 2010, in a very special place where ancient ceremonies had been performed for decades by the traditional peoples to honor the mother, the father and the child. It was also a place of ceremony to honor the seven seas and the blue path. This Crystal was placed inside the Earth in a powerful leyline in a very special ceremonial spot to honor the way of the sacred waters; as well as to awaken the deeply honored feminine and to respect the gentle and loving energies of the Lemurian people. The Islander people of our planet today are the descendants of the Lemurian people.

Still to this day it is easy to see how wonderful the balanced masculine and feminine energies are in the people. I hardly know of a more gentle, loving, open and welcoming people. The Islands themselves feel soft like a mother's touch, or when angry, a woman's wrath. The Islands are a place where you simply cannot deny the presence of the Sacred Feminine.

Sweden

The fourth of the powerful Crystals was placed in a very special location in the forests of Sweden, which represents the peoples of the North. This Crystal was also placed in a very strong leyline and was given to the "breadbasket of the world," or: "the prophesied people of the North" who would lead the world by their example in returning to a spiritual and awakened way of being. The ceremony was a wonderful one with people from all over the North participating in placing the Crystal deep within the Earth; filled with the prayers for awakening the human consciousness. As the Sami Grandmother sang the ancient songs and drummed the unforgotten rhythms, our hearths were filled with limitless joy and wonder for our Mother Earth and all of her children. Again, you can read in depth about these powerful ceremonies in my first book: "Message for the Tribe of Many Colors."

Since that time and now the three remaining Sacred Crystals and the special Healing Crystal have all been placed into the Earth at their designated locations. It has been one of the greatest honors of my life to place these sacred and deeply honored crystals back into Mother Earth for the healing of humanity and the strengthening of the earth's energy grid.

Egypt

The fifth Sacred Crystal that was given back to our Beloved Mother Earth was the one that we took to Egypt in 2011. Being in Egypt, was a crazy, emotional experience of extreme ups and downs. The amount of poverty, imbalanced masculine and feminine energies, the treatment of animals, children, women and the exuberant amount of pollution are just a few reasons why this trip was energetically, emotional and physically heartbreaking. The lows were very low, but the highs were INCREDIBLE!

Egypt is a fascinating place with so much vibrant history. Still to this day the pyramids that dot the land bring us a sense of wonderment, intrigue and puzzlement. It would take many lifetimes to truly explore and learn from all that there is to explore and understand. It is a place that has baffled scientists and has created arguments between many historical, religious and spiritual people. We are told that the pyramids were built around 2,500 BC. However, I believe they are much older. When you start to study these magnificent creations, you begin to wonder how they were built and for what purpose. The Great Pyramid covers 13 acres (52,609 m2) and has over 2.3 million stones, each weighing up to 200 tons.

For the Great Pyramid to be built in the 20 years "as most historians believe" would mean that every man, woman and child at that time would have to quarry, cut, lift and move then fit a block "so perfectly and tightly that a razor blade cannot fit between them" every 2 and a half minutes for 12 hours each day, 365 days a year! This is simply absurd! So is the idea that these Great Pyramids were built as tombs. We also know that not one mummy has ever been found inside these pyramids. This is simply a theory that has been widely accepted and has been placed in our history books as though it were fact. The little-known truths about the Great Pyramid are astonishing. For instance, many people have never been taught that the Great Pyramid was built at the exact center of the land mass on Earth and is actually built to 1/500th of a degree to exact North. What makes it even more astonishing is that science claims to have only known about the exact placement of the continents since a mere 600 years ago. We also know that the outer stones of the pyramids are built out of white limestone, containing calcium carbonate, which acts as a perfect insulator. The inner blocks, however, are made of dolomite, which contains magnesium and crystal inside, which conducts electricity! The shafts running inside the pyramid, whether it be in the King's or Queen's Chamber or the underground chambers are all lined with granite (brought from a quarry over 500 miles away) which also act as a conductor of energy. These shafts also contain a slightly radioactive substance that then allows an ionization of the air inside the shafts themselves. The pyramids were literally built just as you would make an electric cable with the insulator on the outside and the conductor on the inside. In order for that wire cable to work you must have a source of energy just as the pyramids must have had a source of energy for them to work. It is a lesser-known fact that a deep underground cistern or chamber lays far beneath the Great Pyramid. I was granted access to this chamber on one of my trips to Egypt. There I witnessed with my own eyes the ancient limestone basin that once flowed with water deep beneath the pyramid.

Anytime you have movement of water along limestone an electrical charge will be created. Here in this ancient room I could clearly see where the flow of water against the limestone walls once created the electromagnetic field of energy that shot up through the shafts into the pyramid. On top of the pyramid was a capstone that is said to have been covered with gold, another powerful conductor of electricity.

The pyramids were certainly not tombs; they were energy making machines! In fact, the Egyptian pyramids are not the only pyramids to have underground water chambers that once created energy. These kinds of chambers have been found in the pyramids and Sacred Sites of Mexico, Peru, Stonehenge, Algeria, India, Pakistan, Thailand, Cambodia and Bolivia. Even though the water has stopped flowing, the energy is still being produced, although on a much lower level. Heat scans by an International project called: "Scan Pyramids" have shown the Great Pyramid of Giza is still generating energy. The more I learned about the pyramids the more fascinating they became, and I found myself totally emerged in learning all I could. One of the most captivating discoveries by a group of mathematicians and scientists was the realization that the Egyptians knew about "the Meter."

You might be asking yourself "what is so amazing about the Egyptians knowing about the meter?" You might be surprised to know the length of the meter depends on a precise measurement of the circumference of the Earth, which scientists say we only discovered in 1793! This astonishing discovery leads us to uncover even more interesting facts about how precisely the pyramids were built. For instance, if you take the surface of the four sides of the Great Pyramid divided by the surface of the base you will end up with the golden ratio or Phi (Fibonacci in Math and in nature). If you divide the half diameter with the total height, you get the golden number squared. If you divide the height of the pyramid by its base you get Pi, 3.14 (the circumference of a circle in relation to its diameter). The radius of the base is identical to the height of the pyramid. Again and again when we look at how the pyramid was built, we can continually see the use of Pi, Phi, the golden ratio, even within the inner chambers of the pyramid. If you were to draw a circle on the inside of the circumference of the pyramids base and subtract that length from a circle drawn around the outside of the pyramids base circumference, you will get 299,792458 m/s = the speed of light! Even more mind-blowing is that the length of two sides of the Great Pyramid is also the average distance any point of the equator travels through space in one second! How did our ancient ancestors know all this? It is almost unfathomable, yet there it is in all of its glory waiting patiently for mankind to understand once again.

The pyramids of our planet are filled with mysteries and were built with a higher intelligence than we have been capable of understanding for so long. Gradually, it seems that we are finally waking up to the great mysteries that have been hidden. When we begin to study the ancient pyramids and their placements around the globe, we begin to see something very interesting. If we were to begin marking each Sacred Site on a globe starting with Easter Island or Rapa Nui, home to the sacred Moai stone statues (which, by the way, weigh over 82 tons each and are said to have walked into place); then head east to mark the amazing Paracas drawings and the Nazca lines, Ollantaytambo and its temple of the Condor in the Sacred Valley, Machu Pichu, the underground tunnels and megalithic structures in Cusco such as Sacsayhuaman and the Paratuari pyramids; then crossing the South Atlantic, we can mark Mali and the lands of the Dogon tribe who have known the exact location of the star Sirius B for thousands of years. We can continue over to Algeria with one of the most important sites for early drawings, paintings, and art work in Tassili n'Ajjer. In Egypt, we can mark Siwa and the Great Pyramid of Giza. Further on to Petra, Jordan, Ur in Iraq, Persepolis in Iran, Mohenjo Daro in Pakistan, the Khajuraho temples in India, Pyay in Myanmar, Sukhothai in Thailand, Angkor Wat and Preah Vihear in Cambodia, and then we find ourselves back to the most isolated place on earth, Easter Island. As we look at these pyramids and sacred ancient sites marked on our map or globe, we begin to see that they are all on the same meridian, creating a circle around our planet!

Pyramids have fascinated people, young and old, for millennia, not just because they were a major feat for human technology and a grand cultural achievement but also because of their ability to instill a sense of wonder and possibility. Who were our ancient ancestors? How did they come to obtain such vast amounts of knowledge and how in the world did we, their descendants, lose it?

I have been asking myself these questions for years and my fascination with the pyramids of the world has grown stronger now that I have visited so many of them. The first time I went to Egypt you couldn't imagine my excitement to see the Nile River and the massive pyramids I had only read about or saw on television. As I said before it was a crazy mixture of great highs and lows. My mind couldn't have imagined the level of pollution in the Nile River and on its banks, or the starving animals pulling carts, the unbreathable air and the lack of women walking around. Then there was this brilliant, unbelievable, most awe inspiring moment of standing in front of the Great Pyramid, looking over my shoulder and seeing the Sphinx. My head was spinning. I didn't know whether I wanted to laugh or cry, or simply sit down for the lack of inability to do anything else. My first trip to Egypt was a moment for me to learn and try to comprehend all that I was seeing and feeling. I remember distinctly paying close attention to the different energies at each pyramid and temple as we went down the Nile to visit them. The sites, the sounds, the different cultures and smells, the food and the music all were so new for a woman who grew up in a little farming town in Colorado. Don't get me wrong, I was ready to take it all in and to learn as much as I could from the experience.

The second trip to Egypt started when I knew it was time to take the fifth Sacred Crystal to her new and rightful home. This trip was so special as we traveled with a few people from the first trip whom had become dear friends and a few 'new' people who were meant to be part of the Sacred Ceremony. We spent time and did meditations in many temples like Saqqara, Dahsure, Karnak and Abydos as well as Dendara and the Valley of the Kings and Hatshepsut's Temple, the temples of Edfu and Kom Ombo, the Philae temple in Aswan and the unfinished obelisk. We visited Abu Simbel and Crystal Mountain with the Bedouin people in the White and the Black Desert. We cooked food with them, danced and sang around the fire and even shared in a rainstorm that is said to have never happened in their desert before. The entire trip was an amazing experience, but the highlight of it all was visiting the Great Giza Pyramid once again! When the day finally arrived for us to do the work we were there to do and to perform the ceremony, we were ready!

Our beautiful little group was given special permission to have the entire Giza Plateau to ourselves to do the ceremonies and prayers that were needed to do inside the Great Pyramid. With armed guards stationed outside the entrance, we walked into the pyramid with quiet excitement and reverence, knowing that we had a very important and specific task at hand. We walked up the giant stone steps that lead to the entrance of the Great Pyramid and entered. The air was cool, and it took a few moments for our eyes to adjust to the dim light which showed us the staircase upwards and a little secret passage that leads down. We then separated into three groups, one led by my dear friend Jens, who would take the group representing the balanced masculine up to the King's Chamber, another group led by Joyce would take a group into the underground chamber representing the balanced feminine. Two other very spiritually powerful women and I would be with the Sacred Crystal inside the Queen's Chamber in the center of the pyramid to act as the Oracle or the conductors of the energies between the two other chambers.

I first went with the men up to the top of the pyramid to the King's Chamber and instructed them on what frequency and tones should be used inside to create the highest energetic wave lengths and told them to begin toning in around 15 minutes. I quickly made my way back down the steep staircase to the Queen's Chamber to hand over the Crystal to the two women to hold in the center of the room. Once the Crystal was set in the center of the Queen's Chamber with my two dear friends, their meditation had begun; I had to make my way down to the underground chamber. I began another steep decent down the staircase to the entrance of the pyramid then further down the hidden tunnel that would lead me deep underground. With my legs already shaking from going up and down the intense staircases mixed with the adrenalin created by my own excitement; I began my journey down. In order to get to the underground cistern I had to get down on my hands and knees and begin to follow a very, very narrow tunnel deep into the earth.

With my head tucked to my chest and my back touching the top of the tunnel, shoulders pressed against each side of the etched earth and my hands and knees in the dusty soil, I began my long journey down, down, down the narrow slope. With no way to turn around and no way of knowing where the dark tunnel would end I had to just keep my wits about me and keep moving forward. I remember at one point thinking to myself: "At some point I should be able to hear the group talking to each other," but I couldn't hear anything at all, nor could I see any sign of light at the end of the tunnel. Now, I am not the kind of person to get spooked or scared of the dark or of unknown situations, but I have to admit, being in that tight of a space and that deep in the Earth, in a dark tunnel that you cannot back out of or turn around in at the base of a ancient pyramid was a little challenging. After several minutes of crawling in the dark as quickly as I could, I finally made out a faint light at the end of the tunnel and made my way to the edge where I could lower myself down into the hollowed out space to find the little group of women already in a circle meditating in preparation.

I quickly began to tone with different sounds in order to find the correct frequency and vibration needed to ignite the energy inside the chamber. Once I was able to find the exact tone I realized I had an enormous climb ahead of me to get back to the Queen's Chamber to begin the ceremony, and I was running out of time. I jumped back up into the narrow tunnel and began crawling as fast as I could up the steep incline. My legs and arms were shaking uncontrollably by the time I was able to stand and get a look up at the enormous staircase I had to climb in front of me, in order to take my place in the Queen's Chamber. That was when I heard it..... All at once this sound, this deep earth shaking sound began out of nowhere. It was as if I was standing next to a train thundering down an invisible track all around me. My whole body could feel this deep, loud rumble. I remember turning in a circle as if to look for someone else who could also hear what I was hearing. I was stunned for a moment, and then I realized what it was. It was the three groups of people toning at the same time! It was the most incredible sound I ever heard! It shook my whole body from my inner core to my fingertips, even the hair on the back of my neck and arms were standing on end. I stood there for a moment bewildered at the power of what was taking place and then in a flash I remembered I also had a job to do and I was not in the place I needed to be.

With new-found energy, I practically ran up the staircase and entered the Queen's Chamber to see the two beautiful women face to face, holding a Crystal above their heads, between them toning with every ounce of energy they had in them. I stood next to them and placed my hands over the Crystal and began toning the harmony and frequencies I had been instructed to tone. I do not remember having any thoughts during this time, just pure concentration on the sounds, the tones, energies and frequencies that needed to be offered. I do remember feeling as though the Crystal didn't weigh anything at all. I cannot tell you how long we toned. It was as if time stood still. Then just as suddenly as it had all began, it stopped. No one gave a signal for it to end, there was no timer set, but all at once every single person just stopped toning. There was no trail off of sound, we all just stopped at the exact same moment and it was over. We were finished with the task we set out to accomplish. The three of us in the Queen's Chamber lowered our arms, our knuckles white from holding the Crystal so tight in our hands looked at each other and began to cry. It was such an overpowering feeling of emotion, exhaustion and exhilaration that we were a bit beside ourselves.

In that moment, I felt so much love for these two women, as though I had known them my entire life and loved them like sisters. We hugged each other and wiped away our sweat and tears then went to find the other groups. We went to the staircase to find each group making their way towards us. It was only then that it hit me. How had they all known to start at exactly the same time? The chambers are so far apart that there is no way one group could hear the other, but they did it. They started at the exact second as the other group started. We gathered together at the exit to the pyramid and hugged each other and shared with each other our own experiences. We then slowly made our way outside and down the giant stone steps. It was then that I noticed the armed guards had moved together and were looking at us with enormous eyes. One of them stood in place while the others began to walk backwards still looking at our group with this curious look of bewilderment. The one standing in place just looked at me and asked: "What did you guys do in there?" I took a few steps towards him to answer, and he backed away from me as I approached. I was confused at their reaction and replied that we had just been doing some prayers and a little meditation with toning. The guard who held his place said that he had also heard a loud sound coming from the pyramid and at the moment the sound began; three falcons started to circle the top of the pyramid. I was relieved at his answer, having thought we were in trouble for something we had done. He asked again while walking backwards with giant steps. This time with more curiosity and a little bit of astonishment while pointing up to the pyramid: "Really, what did you guys do in there?"

I looked up at the giant pyramid looming over us as he waved me back towards the group of guards. Then I saw it for myself. The pyramid was glowing! It was undeniably glowing! There was a white light surrounding the pyramid and it seemed to pulse like a heartbeat with the light growing on each pulse. We all started to walk backwards with our eyes on the pyramid and our mouths gaping wide open to get a better look. None of us could really believe our eyes. Even when it was time to get back on the bus and go back to the Luxor hotel we all had our faces pressed to the windows trying to comprehend it all as we moved further away from the pyramid. Once we got to the hotel, we gathered in the dining area with windows facing the pyramid. It was astonishing to say the least; some of us couldn't even speak, and others were so excited, they couldn't stop speaking, but for all of us it was a life-changing experience. We sat and watched the Great Pyramid of Giza glow! To our astonishment the next day the second and third pyramid also begun to glow!

The next few days were just as exciting, now that the work was done in the Great Pyramid; we needed to prepare ourselves for the second and final crystal ceremony. We had taken this Sacred Crystal with us into every pyramid and temple along the Nile, each giving its own special blessing and information to the Crystal for the time of its return to the Mother. By the time we had arrived in Alexandria, we were all ready to take part in the final ceremony. There, on the beautiful beach where the Nile river flows into the ocean, we stood ceremoniously in the formation that is symbolic to the Great Pyramids themselves and a configuration that can be found in our heavens above. We stood in the formation of the constellation of Orion or, to the Egyptians, Osiris and began the ceremony to reignite the ancient energy and wisdom of the many temples and pyramids we had visited and to reunite the sacred energy grid of our ancestors. Giving our thanks to the four directions, our ancestors and the wisdom they carried, along with our own personal prayers for humanity to move into love in order to understand these ancient truths and the unseen wisdom, we prepared the Crystal to go back home. When the ceremony was complete and all the prayers were said and heard, I asked my dear friend Jens, who had led the group in the King's Chamber to represent the healed masculine and my wife Joyce who represented the healed feminine in the underground chamber, to be the carriers of the Crystal.

This Sacred Crystal was to be placed in a very specific place, "where the Nile goes to rest in the Mediterranean." So with one final closing prayer on the quiet beach in Alexandria I said my final goodbye to the Sacred Crystal and handed Her over to Jens and Joyce. These two strong swimmers representing the balanced masculine and feminine swam far out into the turquoise waters then let Her float down into her new beautiful watery home.

Japan (The Healing Crystal)

I was in Wales getting ready to walk out onto the stage to give a lecture, when a friend popped out from behind the curtain and whispered in my ear that a tsunami had just hit Japan destroying a nuclear power plant. At the time, none of us could have imagined just how terrible this tragedy would be for our beautiful planet, but as the days went on and we all watched this disaster unfold on our television screens the reality of it began to sink in. It didn't take long for me to understand exactly where the Sacred Healing Crystal that was given to me had to go. We had to go to Japan!

I began asking people from around the world to send crystals filled with healing prayers and intentions to help delete radiation for our brothers and sisters in Japan. It wasn't long before our home was filled with boxes and boxes of crystals. Our friends in Japan were also amazed at how many crystals were being sent directly to them as their rooms were also being filled.

In the spring of 2014, we found ourselves walking into the airport with several very heavy, very full suitcases all filled to its capacity with crystals. On arriving in Tokyo, we met our beautiful little Japanese group, then we all quickly boarded the next plane heading for the Island of Okinawa.

There we began the first of many healing ceremonies for the ocean as well as the waterfalls and streams in the high country which supply the drinking water for the population. We visited the ancient ceremonial sites of the Ryukyuan people and offered many healing crystals and prayers to the water. Once our work was completed on the Island of Okinawa, it was time to head for the southernmost inhabited Island in Japan. We were about to go to the little island of

Yonaguni and the home of the amazing underwater pyramid!

With great excitement, our little group filed our way into the tiny bright yellow airplane. We sat happily eating our boxed lunches to the sound of the propellers roaring away, as we crossed the East China Sea. When we finally got a closer look at the island, we noticed right away that the landing strip was about the same size as the island itself! We all gave each other a few exciting glances then strapped ourselves in and prepared for landing.

Stepping out of such a funny little airplane and onto such a remote island I felt for just a fleeting moment as if I were Robinson Crusoe on an epic adventure. We were greeted by a beautiful local man who shuttled us to our little hotel (perhaps the only hotel on the island). Later in this trip, it turned out that this same man was also our waiter, our driver, our musical entertainer for the days on the island and our guide on the boat! The small population of people living here were so kind and so happy living, eating and singing just as their ancestors had done for hundreds and hundreds of years. We visited the ancient burial tombs and were shown some of the most ancient forms of writing known to man. We explored the island and saw extraordinary plants and trees, many of which only grow on that island. We even got the privilege of getting up close to a rare band of wild horses that lived atop the highest part of the island. Every moment was a rich and wonderful experience, but we were all waiting with considerable excitement to see the great underwater pyramid! When the moment finally arrived, we took a little boat out onto the ocean with the man who discovered the pyramid. Along with many crystals in our pockets, we began our ceremonies on the water. We prayed to the four directions and the four elements, to Great Spirit and Mother Earth, then prayed for the healing of our waters before offering crystals (from ourselves and from all over the world) to the water. It was a powerful ceremony, not only because the boat was filled with the people from Japan, all so desperately wanting to be kept safe from the radiation ravishing their land and water, but also because we were directly over the underwater pyramid laying just a few meters under us. It was so special to have this Healing Crystal in my hands knowing that it was forever connected to the other Sacred Seven and now it was connecting to this ancient hidden pyramid.

Once our prayers were finished, we were guided to the bottom of the glass-bottomed boat where we could clearly see the ancient structure, the cut walls, stone blocks and chiseled staircase as well as a huge sun dial and in the distance, what looked like a Moai head from Easter Island! The place was simply amazing and the amount of energy that could be felt coming from the pyramid was so strong, it left the hairs on our arms standing straight up. Even the crystals that we dropped into the water were glowing with every imaginable color possible.

With this extraordinary experience forever in our hearts and minds, we reluctantly left the Island of Yonaguni and headed for Tokyo where I would be giving several lectures to the Japanese people in order to teach them about the importance of using crystals. Each day we passed out crystals to the people that had been sent from all over the world to help delete radiation and help heal with their energy. On the last day of the many events, I brought out the Sacred Healing Crystal for all of the people in attendance to connect to; where they could offer their own prayers and blessings before the final ceremony was performed. When the lectures and events were all over we furthered our journey by heading to Yamanashi and then on to Nagano. In each town where we stopped, we passed out crystals to the people and taught them how to use them. We offered prayers, crystals and ceremonies at each sacred well, stream, river and lake accompanied by the local female Elders in each area. Soon we were in the mountains of Yatsugatake where the hillsides were covered in the beautiful pink cherry blossoms. We visited ancient temples, sacred forests, and revered giant trees where we prayed for the land, the people and the water.

After a day of rest and soaking in the mountain's natural hot springs we were all ready and anxious for the big day to have finally arrived. We started our day's journey pretty high up in the mountains. However, we wanted to be able to go to the top, to the source of the river that flows all the way down into its many different branches of rivers, streams, canals and lakes before emptying itself into the sea. As we went higher and higher in elevation, the temperature got colder and colder. Soon we found there was ice and snow still lining the banks of the river. Knowing I had to place the Crystal deep into the water, the ice was not a very welcoming sight at all. When we knew we had gone as high as we possibly could go I began looking for the best place for us to gather along the river. I spotted a large boulder that had fallen from the cliff side and landed in the icy water. This was a perfect spot for the new home of the Sacred Crystal.

The constant rush of water flowing against the face of the boulder created a deep impression in the earth at its base under the water, leaving an area I could wedge the Crystal under so it couldn't be removed. With the beautiful Healing Crystal in my hands, I began the ceremony. Several of the Elders from a neighboring village down below, also made the trek up to the top of the mountain, to give their prayers, their songs and their blessings to the Crystal. We were a beautiful group, lined along the bank of the river all saying our most heartfelt prayers for the blessing and cleaning of the waters and the deletion of radiation. It was an emotional moment to say the least. These beautiful people were literally living in the midst of an unprecedented radiation disaster. Family members and loved ones being directly affected. Their prayers were heartbreakingly raw, and their words filled with such devotion left me in tears. The Elders and I said our last few prayers before I held the Crystal in my hands and walked towards the water. Joyce, never leaving my side, helped me hold the Crystal tightly as we walked straight into the icy water. We tried to stay as focused as possible on what we were doing; not giving attention to the stabbing cold that was literally taking our breath away. Once the water was up to our chest, and I was close enough to the giant boulder, I took one last breath and went under. With a few adjustments of smaller stones under the boulder I was able to wedge the Sacred Healing Crystal in tight, and then come up for air. This was when I became aware of just how hard my body was trying to fight to adjust to the temperature. I tried to take a breath in but I just couldn't; I opened my mouth to breathe in but my breath was just gone. Joyce grabbed my hand and began finding the quickest way out of the water between the rocks and pulled me up onto the bank. While I tried to recover, Joyce and a few others distributed the rest of the crystals that had been sent from all over the world for this moment, to the rest of my beautiful Japanese group along the bank. To my utter surprise, with tears running down their faces, praying with all their hearts, they too began to walk straight into the icy water to offer their crystals. The image of these wonderful people standing in the freezing water, praying with all their might, in total humility and authentic dedication is something I will never forget.

To this day, the radiation from the Fukushima plant continues to pour radioactive fallout into the Pacific Ocean. This event is unprecedented in its total release of radioactive contamination into our ocean and up until now it's still happening! Although the radiation is still flowing into our oceans and is found in our food and our drinking water around the world, there are things we can do to protect ourselves. Remember to wear a Crystal around your neck and to place one in the refrigerator as well as a container that holds your drinking water; install these Crystals with prayers to delete radiation (NOT absorb, but delete).

The Netherlands

It was late December 2012, when my life seemed to break into little puzzle pieces, and I had to scramble to put it all back together. I was lying on the couch in sunny Santa Fe New Mexico waiting for Joyce to call and tell me when her flight would land in the States after a visit to see her parents in The Netherlands. When the phone rang I was surprised to hear it wasn't Joyce, but it was the landlord of the house I was renting telling me: "We are sorry but we decided to sell the house, and you have two weeks to move out." My mind was racing trying to figure out what in the world I was going to do when the phone rang for the second time. This time it was Joyce and there was definitely something wrong. Somewhere between being in shock, heartbroken and worried, she uttered the words: "I can't come home." Through her tears, she explained that she was being deported, her passport had been taken and given to the pilot, and she was being put back onto the plane by security to The Netherlands because our marriage was not valid in America. Then the phone was taken from her and the call was ended. Just like that, in five minutes time, my life went from normal to upside down.

The next two weeks were a blur of emotions; from absolute panic to being sick with worry and the fear of the unknown. The only option for me was to move to The Netherlands. If I wanted to live with my wife, I had two weeks' time to box up what I could send and sell everything else before I had to turn in the house keys. Shutting off credit cards, home and health insurances, phone lines, electric, water and sewer, selling my vehicle, furniture and anything else that could not fit into a UPS box was a mind-numbing experience. But to be honest it was easier than trying to expedite all of the legal paperwork needed to move me and my son to a new country. In that same two-week period and on the other side of the ocean, Joyce had to find a job, find a place for us to live and buy a car; and we had to find all of this in a town endowed with an International school for my son Jordan.

By the time my son and I arrived in The Netherlands my nerves were completely shot, all of the anxiety of leaving home and everything I ever knew started to catch up with me, and I simply broke down. Joyce's beautiful parents were truly the sweetest, trying their best to speak English and making us feel right at home. They cooked us wonderful meals and treated us like family. Their genuine love and care was so pure; it was like having your favorite and familiar blanket as a little kid while being in a new place. They drove us around and helped us figure out everything from what fridge we needed to buy to renting a trailer to transport beds to our new place in Maastricht, a city in the very south of the country. Having mama helping us clean and paint and papa installing shelves and hooking up the washing machine, sharing a cheese sandwich and chit chatting like any family would do, was simple, familiar, normal and just what I needed. To this day, I do not think they realize it was them who made it all alright for me to have left everything and everyone I had ever known. They brought a sense of family and a feeling of home, of calm and peace to the chaos. They had become my blanket. That first couples of weeks in The Netherlands were very hard, everything was a first and all was happening so fast. The reality that I had literally left my old life and had to start completely over from ground zero was a daunting feeling. Some days were ok while I kept myself busy, other days were much harder.

On one of the last nights we stayed with Joyce's parents

before moving into our own home, I went to the backyard and began to say my nightly prayers. Before I knew it, my emotions got the best of me and everything came flooding out. The reality set in that I was in a complete different country and there would be no "going back home," like all my other trips. The home I knew was gone, my things and the normalcy of what I defined my life with was gone, and I didn't know anyone. The city was so big and there were so many people and streets, cars, bikes and sounds. I couldn't understand the language, and my son was going into a big school. I had to just trust he would adjust and my daughter… my daughter…. The thought itself was almost too much to bear and the pain too real, too raw and too much for me to physically and mentally cope with. Although the court separated the kids during the divorce, and she was happily living with dad; I also knew I had only been given summers and holidays with her; how could I be ok with this? Why was my life taking this journey? Why The Netherlands? What was the purpose of all of this?

My prayers were more sobbing incoherent words than structured sentences with the up welling of so much grief when all of a sudden... out of nowhere…, I saw in my mind's eye the Sacred Crystal that was given to The Netherlands earlier that year. I could see it clear as day, every line and detail, every fracture of light hitting it as though it was lit up by the sun. While seeing this beautiful Crystal in my mind, I began to remember the Sacred Ceremony and placing the Crystal into the Earth of The Netherlands. In some weird way, I knew in that moment this Crystal and I shared some special connection, something unique and unbreakable. That it, just like me, had spent its entire life in the Americas and then one day, out of the blue, had crossed the ocean to find its new home in this country, where it would complete its most important work. I stood there in the darkness of my in-laws' backyard in total silence, being completely overwhelmed by the imagery of the Crystal and remembering when I first realized it had to go to The Netherlands.

I was still living in Santa Fe on the day I was told where the sixth Sacred Crystal had to go. It was a moment that is hard to describe but also a very familiar one to me. It was the feeling of the body getting heavy and the tactical sense of warm water being poured from the top of my head down to my feet. In those moments, I know something is going to happen. Either I will hear The Great Mothers' voice, or I will be shown something. This time I was given the location of where the Crystal had to go. It was not a guess; it was not a suggestion, a proposition or a recommendation by any means. It was an absolute and unshakable knowing. The Crystal would be given to The Netherlands.

Just as quickly as the experience had happened, it had gone, and I was left sitting there in my backyard watching the sun go down over the hills to the west thinking to myself: "The Netherlands? But..., why The Netherlands?" To be completely honest I didn't want to mention this to anyone, I didn't even tell Joyce for some time because it just didn't make sense to me. Crystals were always given to indigenous or Sacred lands, and always in the wilderness away from people, so again..., why this densely populated country?

After several weeks of thinking about this and trying to come up with some explanation or solution to the problem, I still had no answer. One, the Crystal must be placed inside a powerful leyline; two, it must be placed in nature away from people, paths, interruptions of any kind; and three, each Crystal represents something Sacred in particular. So again, why The Netherlands? As far as I could tell there were no indigenous people from The Netherlands nor Sacred Sites that I was aware of, other than religious chapels, cathedrals and holy wells. Then I found out about the Megalithic sites such as the dolmens, the so-called "Hunebedden". There are 53 megalithic monuments scattered over the landscape in the north of the country with granite stones weighing up to 20 tons that have been placed there some 5,500 years ago as burial chambers. After a lot of prayer, I knew this was not the place or the purpose of the Crystal going to The Netherlands. The more I researched the more perplexed I became about it.

It took several months before the answers would come as to why The Netherlands would be receiving the sixth Sacred Crystal, and those answers had nothing to do with indigenous peoples or a particular Sacred Site. The answer was WATER! The Crystal that would be given to The Netherlands was for the purpose of blessing the water. The Dutch relationship with water is unlike that of any other country in the world! One-third of the Dutch territory is actually below sea level and during the centuries reclaimed by the people themselves, while another third is at zero measuring level. Not only are most of the cities built around canals, The Netherlands also holds the densest network of waterways in all of Europe. In Amsterdam alone there are more than one hundred kilometers of canals, 90 islands, 1,500 bridges and is considered to be the Venice of the North. You simply cannot think of The Netherlands without thinking of water. Water is everywhere and water as we know, is the lifeblood of our planet. It is revered as our most vital and life-giving element and the container of those little miracles we call Crystals.

We know that water is not only a sacred living energy, but it has the capacity to absorb, carry and respond to our intentions. We also know that the energy of our thoughts and feelings are not only contained inside our bodies or our minds; they are also shared and spread through an electromagnetic field when two or more people share their energy of desires, love, prayers and gratitude; those energies will multiply, creating a collective field of vibration and resonance that can affect the water around us. Understanding how our conscious thoughts and prayers, our emotions and our gratitude has an effect on the water, there no longer existed any doubt in my mind to the reasons why the Sacred Crystal was being called home to The Netherlands.

Although I now understood why the Sacred Crystal had to go to The Netherlands, I still had no idea about the exact location. I had to find a place undisturbed by humans, away from any activity and where water and major leyline would be present. Secondly, the Crystal needed to contain our collective prayers and energy before being placed. So while I searched and prayed for the right location to be given, a dear friend from "Heart for Earth" began the giant task of gathering the spiritual people from The Netherlands and abroad together for a very special ceremony in Rotterdam, for the purpose of give our prayers and energy to the Crystal.

It became a gathering unlike anything I had ever experienced before. Over 1,500 people lined up ready to enter the huge church called Sint-Laurenskerk in Rotterdam. The church itself is an amazing building, being the only surviving remnant of the medieval city that was destroyed by the German air force in World War II in 1940. I remember the feeling of great excitement and a strange feeling of anxiety as I watched how many people were coming to give their love and blessings to the Sacred Crystal. I have spoken to many crowds and on many stages all over the world but this truly was unlike anything I had ever seen. Standing on the stage holding the Sacred Crystal in a protective leather pouch I looked out over the crowd to see every race, color and ethnic background ready and present to do their part for our beautiful Mother Earth. I remember so clearly having a moment of the purest pride in humanity, for our unwavering yearning to essentially do good and to be good in order to make this world a better place.

Children filled the floor in front of me with anticipation and smiles on their faces; others filled every chair and stood in every available space along the walls. There were disabled people in wheelchairs and even a person in a hospital bed. Young and old were all present to pray for our Mother Earth. It was a moment I will never forget and still to this day it brings tears to my eyes. Throughout our history, there have been many struggles and many moments in which people had to make a stand for something, whether it be political, religious or ethical. On this day, we were making the greatest stand of all; we stood for the unity of human kind and for the protection and love of our Great Mother Earth. We prayed as one in all of our many different ways. We offered our own individual prayers and blessings for the healing of our planet and all humanity. We joined as one as children of Mother Earth in love and gratitude. We were no longer American or Dutch; we were no longer white or black, yellow or red; we were not male or female, and we were not rich or poor. We were family; we were brothers and sisters of one Mother, standing for one purpose. We truly were "the Tribe of Many Colors." The prophesied tribe that would gather together as one people to create the greatest change on earth and begin the movement from ego into love consciousness.

Before the ceremony was over, I stood and walked with

the Crystal over my head through the many rows of people, letting them all see the Crystal up close. Halfway through the endeavor my arms started to shake, and I struggled to keep them up. I tried to bring my arms down to a different position when I realized my arms had locked into place from holding it above my head for so long. Just when I thought I might drop it, two arms swooped over me from behind and held my arms up. Turning my head, I saw a very familiar face: it was Jens, my dear friend from the Egypt trip and a man I consider to be my heart's brother, standing there with a gentle smile on his face. He held my arms up throughout the rest of the rows of people and helped me back onto the stage where we said the final prayers. The crystal contained not only the prayers from the people inside the church but also the prayers offered from the thousands who had tuned in on live stream from around the world.

Once the closing prayers were finished the milky white Sacred Crystal turned bright white in my hands. It literally radiated light and turned as hot as fire to the touch. I had to hold a leather pouch between the Crystal and my hands in order to place it back inside. I have seen many amazing things happen with Crystals, from them turning so hot to the touch that you cannot hold them, to glowing with the brightest light and even spinning up off the ground while emanating all manner of colors. I have been very blessed to experience the miracles of Crystals so many times in the last eight years. My awe and amazement in them will never cease to exist.

Once the gathering in Rotterdam was over and the prayers of thousands had been given to the Crystal, it was time to place the Crystal in its new home so that those prayers could be spread through the leylines energy and the waters memory.

Finding this special place was the hardest task of the entire project. The answer came in the most unpredictable way. Joyce and I were walking through an airport coming home from a lecture abroad when we got a phone call, a call that would change everything and stop the endless search for the Crystals new home. A member of the Dutch Royal family was offering to help us and knew of a place that was not only cut off from human activity; it also was in nature and exactly where an extremely powerful leyline runs east to west. The search was over and I could finally gather the small group of people to assist me in placing the Sacred Crystal into the Earth.

When the day finally arrived, the sun was shining, and we gathered at the edge of a secure and secluded path. With bare feet, I walked leading the group waiting to feel exactly where the leyline was running. There really is nothing like the feeling of stepping onto a leyline for me. It is a high vibration that literally makes the soles of my feet vibrate or tingle. The closest thing I could imagine comparing it to is the feeling in your hands after using a power sander for an hour. I walked barefoot for less than a kilometer when I suddenly stepped right onto it. I knew the leyline I was looking for was one of the biggest in the world and had tried to ready myself for when I stepped onto it. I was completely unprepared for the amount of energy this leyline was giving off. It literally took my breath away, and I had to adjust myself for a few moments before I could concentrate enough to begin the ceremony itself. Once we were all gathered around a little circle, we began to pray to the four directions, Great Spirit and the Sacred Mother. There was a representative for children, the mother, the father, the healed masculine and feminine as well as the grandmother and grandfather. A precious friend of mine brought soil from every province of The Netherlands as well as a gift from the Dalai Lama with his blessings. There were gifts of flower petals, sage and sweet grass as well as water I had gathered from sacred places around the world, all to be placed in the ground with the Sacred Crystal. The prayers were said, and the beloved Crystal went into its new damp earthly home where the prayers would be shared throughout the leyline energy grid and with the countless water Crystals in The Netherlands and to the rest of the world.

The last thing I remember thinking about was saying the closing prayer and placing the last handful of soil onto where we buried the Sacred Crystal.

Then, just like that, I found myself pulled back out of my thoughts and realized I was standing once again fully present in the backyard of Joyce's parents' house. I was left wondering why in the middle of my heartbroken prayer did I just relived the entire experience of the Dutch Crystal. The slow realization came to me, that just as I had no idea why one of the Sacred Crystals was meant for The Netherlands; it did not mean it was wrong; it was just unknown. I could not see the bigger picture when I was sitting in America asking myself: "Why The Netherlands?" Now I was finding myself in the same exact position feeling anxious and worried and wondering why I was in The Netherlands? It was in that moment that I could actually breathe again and let some of my worries and questions go, knowing that everything has a purpose and a reason even if I did not know what they were yet. Just like the Crystal, I had flown across the ocean and left what was familiar behind to begin my new life, in a new place, a new home, The Netherlands.

Today, years later, I can see that Joyce being deported was not a tragedy, nor was it just a cruel suffering we were meant to go through. It was a very clever move by Great Spirit and Mother Earth. They knew I would follow my beloved wife to the ends of the Earth to be with her and The Netherlands was where they wanted me to be. I couldn't see back then that by moving to The Netherlands I would find the dearest friends I have ever had and I would be free of several serious illnesses I have had for so many years caused by fear, suppression, anxiety and shame. I still have to shake my head in almost utter disbelief, when I think of the immense shifts I have made in my life. I have gone from being a Mormon housewife in an all Mormon village, feeling I was wrong and unworthy to the core of my being for who I was and what I believed in; feeling like an outcast to all the people I once knew; to now living the most blessed life one can imagine. The kindness, the acceptance, the little village I live in and the beautiful people living here have changed my life. I live my life with pride in my family and pride in the place I call home. I live my life's purpose without worrying about criticism or shame and without hate or bitterness for being who I am, loving who I love and believing what I believe in. I am happy and I am healthy and most importantly; I have LOVE.

Peru (Lake Titicaca)

It had been eight years since the moment I was entrusted with the seven Sacred Crystals. I experienced many adventures around the world, sacred ceremonies and epic journeys to find the homes for the Crystals. Now I was left with just one. It was an exciting moment to finally know with clarity where the seventh and final Crystal would be going to, to complete the energetic grid around the world. I was going to Peru, to Lake Titicaca!

Lake Titicaca is the largest lake in South America and the highest lake in the world, located over 12.500 feet (3.810 meters) above sea level. It is a place surrounded by mysteries and ancient stories and to me; it is one of the most fascinating places on the planet.

Peru and Lake Titicaca are places I remember learning about in fifth grade, sitting at my little wooden top desk with the teacher pointing to its location on the map that had been pulled down in front of the chalk board. Images of Lamas, pan flutes, colorful dresses and stone ruins on the hillsides filled my imagination. For a little Mormon girl in a tiny country town, this was a place that only existed on the other side of the world or could have just as easily been a fairy tale. So many years and experiences later I was packed and ready to board the plane for Lima Peru with the last of the Sacred Crystals under my arm!

It was surreal, almost incomprehensible that I was actually going to Peru. It had been a dream of mine for so long that it all seemed a bit unreal until we spotted our first glimpse of the snow-covered peaks of the Andean Mountains out of the airplane window. At that point, it finally hit me, we were really doing it! I was actually seeing the Andes! Joyce and

I looked at each other, then burst into excited giggles. In no time, we had landed in Lima and made our way to baggage claim and the exit doors. The automatic doors slid opened and to my surprise, there was a crowd gathered screaming and waving and trying to take photos before the door closed. I looked around with a bit of bewilderment, the room we were in was all but empty with the exception of me Joyce, Jordan, our friend Tom and a young Peruvian boy. The door opened again with the same excitement, cheers and photos being flashed before it closed once more. They knew me in Peru? When the door opened again I did my best to wave and smile as I walked out like a real celebrity, only to find out the little Peruvian teenager behind us was a local pop star! We had a good laugh and climbed into the most amazing, beat up; multi-colored bus with its side door flung wide open. We were bouncing and weaving between the other cars. Our eyes were wide open and our smiles bursting from cheek to cheek. At last, we had officially arrived in Peru! We enjoyed a couple of days off while the others from our group made their way to Lima in order to begin our journey to the different Sacred Sites and to perform the crystal ceremony. After we had all arrived and visibly enjoyed the Lima market, dressed in our newly purchased Peruvian pants, ponchos, and Chullo hats we were ready to fly to Cusco where we would meet our guide and indigenous Andean Shaman, Mallku.

Now, if you have ever been to the Lima airport, you will understand what I'm talking about when I say, the flight's time and schedule are more of a suggestion than an exact intended procedure. We all arrived at the airport very early in the morning with several hours to spare to assure everyone in the group would make their flights from Lima to Cusco, when all of a sudden over the loudspeaker came the announcement that several of us should be boarding immediately! For no explainable reason, a few of us were randomly chosen to board a departing flight. We looked at each other like a couple of deer caught in headlights then jumped into action. Joyce, Jordan and a couple of others sprinted ahead knowing that running was not a possibility for me having just had a broken leg, 6 screws, pins and a metal plate installed, just a couple of months earlier. My darling friend "Momma Mariuza" and Katharine, "the other non-runners in the group" lagged behind with me. We struggled to keep an eye on Joyce's curly dark hair as it bounced ahead of us through the crowd in order to know where we were supposed to go.

Dragging my left leg behind me in a awkward gallop the three of us began our struggle down the long corridors and winding hallways. Through the wheezing, the sweating and the odd comment of "just leave me," "save yourselves" and "I haven't ran since 1970," the three of us finally made it to the boarding gate and fell into the plane. By the time we all had arrived in Cusco, we realized the wheezing had just begun. At an elevation of 11,150 feet (3,399 meters) we were all chewing the Cocoa leaves and drinking extra water to fight off the effects of altitude sickness. From Cusco airport, we traveled by bus with our Incan master Mallku to the much-anticipated Sacred Valley, the epicenter of the Inca culture.

The sight of the valley itself is a unique experience as you leave the high, desert like mountains and slowly make your way into the green fertile fields of flowers and crops below. We stopped at several sacred and powerful spots on our journey with the intention of connecting the Sacred Crystal to each and every Sacred Site beginning with Chinchero, and the Earth Alter. From this special and highly energetic place where we connected to the Sacred Mother Pachamama, we headed for the ancient Inca city of Ollantaytambo, filled with the mysteries of ancient technology and architecture. It is the place of the enormous Sun temple, with its numerous terraces and the ancient princess fountain.

Next we traveled to Moray, the place of amazing Inca circular or spiral terraces that seemed almost supernatural in their perfect construction and location. While we were there we offered prayers to the four directions, to Great Spirit and Mother Earth, each of us representing one of the four directions depending on what country we came from. It was such a powerful ceremony and we were all awakening to the immense importance of what we had come to do. We were not only there to learn the mysteries, the sacredness and the importance of these ancient sites but to also connect our energies with this land and to bring our gift, the last Sacred Crystal, to the Mother. From Moray and the circular terraces, we traveled by train to the village of Aguas Calientes or Machu Picchu, the wonderful and isolated city hidden in the Andes of Peru. It is a place I have wanted to see with my own eyes for so many years! The moment we arrived and stepped out onto the narrow stone street the feeling of being somewhere very special, somewhere hidden from time and unique in every way possible flooded the senses. The air was damp with the lushness of the jungle forest all around us and the smell of wood fires burning. There were huge rock cliffs, which jutted out over the roaring white water rushing down the mountain and even higher mountain peaks, which encircled the little village at their base.

Machu Picchu! There it was, written in big bold letters in front of a giant bronze statue of Pachacutec, the Great Inca Emperor. I wasn't reading these words off of a map or from my fifth-grade history book; I was standing in the middle of the city! Between the tears welling up and the excited giggles of almost utter disbelief, I saw something that literally made me pinch myself. Maybe I was dreaming after all? A huge and completely hairless dog walked in front of me and then was safely escorted across the street by all the local people. I looked at some of the group that were standing with me; they too had the same expression on their face as I did. Mallku soon came walking up to us with a big smile on his face and said: "I see you have seen the Peruvian Hairless dog." I had no idea this kind of dog even existed. I come to find out it is an ancient pre-Incan breed that has even been thought to have had mystical powers. I had not been in the village five minutes, and already I was experiencing things I could not have imagined.

That night we explored the little winding streets and enjoyed some local food, then prepared ourselves for the journey to the ancient ruins. The next morning we were all ready and excited to make our way up the winding narrow road in our buses to the ancient site of Machu Picchu, the ancient city in the sky. This was the moment I had been doing all of my physical therapy for, preparing my leg for the hundreds of stone steps leading straight up to the stone city on top of the mountain. Broken leg or not, I was going up that mountain and there was nothing that could stop me! In every direction one could look, there was jaw dropping beauty. From the flashes of lightning stretching out across the dark blue sky in the distance, the green hillsides of the surrounding mountain peaks, to the ancient ruins glowing with their own energy, it was breathtaking! Our little group first walked high up above the city of Machu Picchu where we could sit on a grass terrace and look out across the ruins.

Here we started our first ceremony and offered our prayers

and our gratitude. We quickly found ourselves overwhelmed by the energy of this special place. As our ceremony came to an end and with one last great flash of lightning, the dark blue clouds broke and a streaming warm light poured down from the heavens lighting up our little group sitting on the side of the mountain. Soon a brilliant rainbow appeared along with butterflies and birds swirling all around us. We found ourselves overcome with joy and gratitude for such an experience. The next two days were spent exploring the city and discovering all of its wonders from the ingenious waterways which brought fresh water up the mountain, to the perfectly cut and placed stones that created the walls and steps (thought to have been built by pre-Incan and Incan people.) We found ourselves in awe of the masterful architecture and sheer effort it must have taken to create the countless terraces used to grow their crops so high on the rocky mountain tops.

We have all seen photos of the ancient city Machu Picchu in a magazine or on a postcard and our eyes always see the stone walls on top of a mountain but what we do not tend to look at is the soil. Yes, the soil. Every ounce of the soil in the city and in the hundreds of agricultural terraces used to grow their crops had to be brought up to the top of the mountain from the fertile valley below! It truly boggles the mind to see such a magnificent place. The experience was just amazing; to be able to stand atop this Sacred Mountain and be surrounded by such ancient sites, one could really get a sense of how intertwined the people were with the Great Mother, Pachamama and how advanced they truly were.

Along a high path, above the ancient site we stopped and gathered in an open cave overlooking the valley opposite Machu Picchu where we did our last and final ceremony to connect the Sacred Crystal to this powerful place and to offer our love and respect before heading back down and continuing our travels. I remember stopping for just a moment to have one more look around so that I would never forget this place or this moment in my life. The ancient city atop the mountain, the river at the bottom of the valley that is the beginning of the great Amazon, the green colored mountain peaks, the dark sky and my lovely group, 35 beautiful people from every corner of the world, my friends, my family, all here because they love their Mother Earth as much as I do. This moment will forever be etched into my mind.

We spent one more night in the beautiful Sacred Valley before we made our way back up into the high desert mountains and the ancient site called Tipon, the Temple of water and the serpent cave. This amazing place showed us the intricate irrigation systems that the Inca had been using for hundreds of years to bring water uphill. We were then off to Q'enqo, the sacred place of the Puma and one of the favorite spots we visited. When we first arrived to this Sacred Site, it looked to be nothing more than huge stones that had been carved in many different places for seating areas. There were also stairs etched into the solid stone along with images of snakes and the symbol of the sacred puma, but the most magical place was what we couldn't yet see from where we were standing. Winding down narrow steps to the base of the large stones, we came to a small entrance into the earth. A room maybe 3 by 6 meters had been carved out of solid stone leaving a large slanted ceiling overhead and along the wall sat an enormous shrine cut from a single stone. Mallku taught us that this was where gifts and prayers were offered to Pachamama. It became the place where our little group did one of the most heartfelt and powerful ceremonies. The songs, toning and prayers that we offered seemed to resonate

not only in the room but deep into the core of each and
every one of us. We truly felt as though we were held by the
presence of the Great Mother as we presented our gratitude
for all the blessings She gives us each day. It was such a
lovely experience to offer our prayers in such a sacred place,
where so many had come before us and had done the same
thing.

When we finally pulled ourselves away from this Sacred
Site, we made our way back to the incredible city of Cusco. It
is a city that makes you feel as though you have been thrown
back in time. There are ancient stone streets and walls built
with such precision you could not put a razor blade between
them. There are ancient cathedrals and plazas filled with
local women wearing colorful dresses and extraordinary
hats carrying bundles of goods on their backs. This amazing
place is known as the cradle of Peru's ancient civilizations
and has been called home to many Andean cultures such as
the Purakas, the Tiwanakus, the Incan people and tonight, by
us. We all needed to have some much-needed sleep before
we continued on to the next several Sacred Sites and we were
all happy to fall into our beds.

The next morning, like clockwork we were back on our
bus and heading to a little Inca village called Pisaq and the
incredible mountain that lay just behind it (considered to
an archaeological treasure in its own right). We filed out of
our bus and were met by the beautiful local women selling
corn on the cob and little trinkets who showed us the way
to the magnificent ruins. Mallku had us gather together in a
little circle as he taught us about the historic area. He then
pointed towards the opposite side of the mountain where we
saw several burial cambers in small caves on the cliffs edge.
Although many had been looted over the centuries, some

were still intact. There was such a feeling of humility and honor to witness such a place and to set among some of the ancient ancestors whose bodies still dotted the land. Mallku led us through a prayer to honor those who had lived their lives in this place, this sacred area that they had created so many years ago. He also taught us about the many, many terraces that we saw, built up along the hillsides surrounding us. How it took several generations to build each one and how each terrace had to be filled with top soil by hauling it up from the valley below in order for them to grow their crops. Normally, crops would not be able to grow at 11,000 feet (3,353 meters), but here as if by magic they do.

We went our own separate ways to explore the sprawling ancient site. Some went up to the top ruins to offer songs and prayers. A few of us went down to the terraces. I went with a couple of people walking down a little path toward the terraces when all of a sudden a little school group of Peruvian village children began to shyly gather around us. For some reason, they were all very inquisitive of us, especially me and my friend Paul. They would giggle then try to convince each other to be brave enough to get closer to one of us. Finally, I took the initiative and broke the ice by walking up to them, smiling and saying hello. Soon Paul and I had several little girls and boys surrounding us, all very, very interested in touching our hair! Eventually, the nervousness was gone, and their cameras came out, each wanting a photo with us. Even the teacher who had brought them wanted his photo taken as well. It was so much fun and such a delight to interact with these children who; we later found out, came from a very remote village and who had never seen someone with yellow hair before or a man as tall as my friend Paul.

Once the group had all come back together and shared

our stories of what we experienced at the site, it was time to move on and make our way to Saqsaywaman. Before we entered the sacred megalithic structures of Saqsaywaman, our beautiful Peruvian guide, Mallku led us on a very narrow path that took us deep between huge standing boulders. In single file, we made our way to what looked like a dead end with enormous walls of stones jutting up all around. This is where he began explaining the sacredness of this spot. This was a place of initiation, a place that would challenge our fears, our self-doubt and ability to rely on the Great Mother. Behind him was a very low, very dark, narrow path that entered inside the massive stone, the entrance to the Sacred Mother. One by one he challenged us to take the initiation ourselves by holding one hand against the right side of the narrow cave entrance and the other hand above our head to protect us from the low ceiling. We had to enter into the total darkness and trust that we would find our way out of the winding cave system.

This was the first time on the trip that we were being challenged to really face some of our deepest fears and surrender to the Mother. It is one thing to talk about trusting the Great Mother and another to really put yourself in a situation where you MUST let go and give over to something greater than yourself. For some of the members of the group, it was simply too much, and they chose not to step into the blackness. Others stood trembling with tears welling up in their eyes but refusing to back down from the challenge. One by one we said our inner prayers and asked the Mother to guide us through the maze of total blackness. A couple of my dearest friends took a deep breath and entered into the cave in silence. I stayed towards the end of the group helping calm the fears of those who were trying to fight their overpowering anxiety of the unknown and darkness. In time, it was my turn, and I would be helping my South African sister who was determined to take the challenge, although shaking uncontrollably.

With one hand on the edge of the narrow opening and the other above my head and hers tightly holding my shoulders, we squeezed through the entrance into the pitch blackness. We were in total and complete darkness feeling our way around the cave wall which winded around in different directions. The ceiling became lower and lower then opened up in some spots while our feet tried to find a secure footing through the loose stones on the ground. The longer it took the tighter the grip became on my back, and I could tell she was starting to panic. I could hear others struggling, even digging at some loose stones trying to find the way out. I could feel my own fear welling up, not because of the darkness but from hearing the others fears coming to the surface, and I, ultimately being responsible for them. At that point, I thought to myself: "Ok, enough is enough, I have to find the way and get my group out of this cave." I began to run my hand down the cave wall to the floor then back up to the low ceiling, then in front of me to feel where to put my feet through the stones on the ground. I could tell that several of the group members got turned around in the blackness and were struggling to keep calm. My dear friends hands on my back were now franticly digging in and her tears of fear were just too much to hold in any longer. Then with a soft warm touch on my shoulder I heard Mallku's voice: "Keep going the direction you are going, you will soon be out." He was there, in the blackness looking after us and when we had done all that we could to find our way out, he was there to guide us the rest of the way. When I could finally feel a slight breeze of air against my skin, I knew we were almost near the exit. With just a few more steps and turns along the cave wall we found the exit. I saw the smiling faces of those who chose not to take the challenge and a couple of faces who made it through the passage all waiting to greet us. That was when I realized just what a challenge it had been for my dear South African friend who just collapsed onto the ground and sobbed.

For many, it was a challenge of a lifetime; for others, it was ok. But as I sat there consoling my sister and hearing the others in the group talking about their experience, I started to realize what a great teaching this initiation was for us all. It had meant something different to all of us. Whether or not we took the challenge or chose to stay behind it was a great reflector of where we were at in our lives. Not one being better than another, by any means, but a great mirror to ourselves of what walls we still have up or have broken down. For me sitting there and pondering the experience I realized, there were so many lessons to be learned from this. How many times throughout our lives, when things get hard, do we simply follow the crowd or believe what others tell us to believe, only to find ourselves just as lost as we did when we started? Then there are times when we need to rely on someone else for help to get us through something. We do not have to have the strength to do it alone. One of the greatest lessons of all was the understanding that when we have done all that we can do for ourselves; something else will always be there to help us through to the finish. I was so grateful for the initiation and so appreciative to be with these beautiful people who were with me and who took on such a challenge.

From the other side of the huge boulders and the initiation cave, we found ourselves gathered together again with a newfound sense of accomplishment and excitement for what was about to come. Mallku led us along a path past open grass hills, stones that had been cut smooth by glaciers and up onto an open hillside. He asked us to close our eyes and to feel our feet on the Sacred Mother and to trust Her once more while walking forward. Step by step, eyes closed we slowly moved forward and then, he said stop. We opened our eyes to see we were standing at the edge of a great cliff. It was magnificent! What we couldn't have known or have seen from where we began the exercise, was that the Great sun Temple and its Megalithic walls were just below us in all its grandeur. Saqsaywaman, one of the most mysterious, mind boggling achievements of mankind!

This ancient place was built by the Kilke culture from around 900 to 1200 AD, prior to the arrival of the Incas. It is a place that creates a profound sense of Awe. There is no other place on Earth that left me with such amazement, curiosity and reverence for the profound knowledge and insight the builders of this place must have had. With the most striking mysteries of architecture, the megalith walls that zigzag back and forth across the land weigh hundreds of tons (the largest being around 300 tons) and are cut and placed with such absolute perfection that even a joint is impossible to see. To this day, we have no evidence of how these stones were cut or even moved. Even the Inca who came much later than the builders of this site had no wheel, no suitable timber or even working domesticated animals. The legends say it was the magic of the Earth and the wish of the stones themselves that allowed them to be transported.

On the upper part of the complex above the giant walls, stood the remains of perfectly geometric shaped foundations for three towers and the house of the sun, as well as the temple of lightning, rainbow, moon and stars. There are also several caves and underground constructions. In its entirety, this place left us speechless, and we were profoundly honored to be witnessing its beauty and feeling its sacred energy. We gathered in the center of the massive open space in front of the megalithic walls and connected our energy and the Crystal's energy to the site, before giving our prayers and gratitude to those who created this place so long ago. With so much to take in and to feel, to contemplate and experience, by the end of the day we were exhausted and ready to head back into the city of Cusco for some much-needed relaxation and a little lighthearted fun.

That Night was October 31st, and it was Halloween in Cusco! The entire plaza was filled with local musicians, parades, street foods and every little Niña and Niño dressed in their colorful costumes. Joyce and I ran quickly to our hotel room to grab the bags of candy I had brought with me. I always like to have treats for the kids wherever I go, a habit that started in Egypt that has just stuck with me. We filled our pockets to the brim and each had as many candies in our hands as we could carry, then we hit the streets! I have never seen such a happy and friendly people, all sharing food and laughter. The children running around and playing with each other. Joyce and I became popular really fast, as soon as the kids figured out we had candy. There was no pushing or grabbing, there were only happy, smiling faces eager to show us their costumes. Shyly they would accept a sucker from us, then off they would go running and laughing again.

It was one of the most memorable Halloweens I have ever had. The day was filled with the ancient and sacred, followed by a night of great fun. It was a magical moment in time spent with my beautiful friends and family in a wondrous country, on an epic journey to help our Mother Earth. What could be better?

After some much-needed sleep, a hot shower and several activated charcoal pills later we were ready for our long seven hour bus ride to the Temple of Wiraqocha. It's never fun to pick up a stomach bug in a far-off country, but it seems no matter how careful I am; I always end up with one at the worst moment possible. Bacterial infection or not, I was on the bus and excited to head out for our next big adventure! As we left Cusco behind us, the landscape became an arid high desert, completely untouched by man except for the little stone houses that dotted the open space along the road here and there. Some with brightly-colored plastic bags tied to the end of tall sticks outside their front doors letting travelers know they had Chicha (an Incan drink made from purple corn) for sale. Now and then we would see a lone farmer plowing his field with ox and plow or a brightly dressed woman carrying bags of goods along the road. Most of the trip was wide-open space where the desert seemed to go on forever until we came to the Raqch'i Wiraqocha Temple. As soon as we arrived at the temple site we noticed that the landscape had changed dramatically. There were hills covered with trees and plant life, even lush wetlands around the large complex that was filled with the sounds of song birds. It was no surprise to find out this temple was a place of sacred springs, fountains, baths and the largest single roof building in the Incan Empire, the Temple of Wiraqocha.

From this amazing place we traveled on, bouncing and winding along on what I would loosely call a road into the city of Puno. It was a great feeling to make it to Puno, knowing that we were so close to finally seeing Lake Titicaca and conducting the ceremony we had all traveled so far to take part in. There was only one more stop we needed to make, one more sacred and magical place we needed to connect ourselves and the Crystal to, the revered Ajayu Marka, otherwise known as the "Gate of the Gods." This breathtaking location is about 241 miles south of Cusco near the shores of Lake Titicaca and one of the most mysterious, sacred places in South America.

The size of the gate itself is about 23x23 feet (7x7 meters), which has been carved out of a solid stone cliff with vertical lines or columns on each side carved into the wall around one foot deep. At the center and ground level of this flat cut wall, there is a lateral door entrance that leads to nowhere. The doorway is inset about a foot deep with a small indention or circular hollow at the center. There is nothing behind the massive door nor is there anything inside it other than solid stone. It reminded me of some of the doorways cut into the cliffs in Petra and in Anatolia Turkey, which are almost identical in size and shape. The local people say that the gate will only open for certain wise people at certain times and is believed to be the place to connect with the Gods. Other theorists say it is for healing the masculine or feminine or that it is a star gate, a portal, or even an energetic source of secret knowledge and power. The Inca legend states that many local shamans watched as the first priest King Aramu Muru placed a golden disk into a recessed area against the doorways' stone wall, after which a kind of gateway opened up and the king disappeared inside never to return.

I do not know exactly what it is, but what I do know is that it is ancient and the creators of this and many of the other sacred megalithic sites were created by absolute masters of intelligence, a people who were deeply connected to Mother Earth. We gathered our group in front of the gateway and said a prayer to connect ourselves and the Crystal with the energy at the site. We each took our separate turns kneeling in the doorway to say our prayers, taking a moment to thank and connect to the creators of this sacred place and their precious wisdom. It was a deeply moving experience to place my heart and my head to the little indentation in the gateway as my ancient ancestors had done before me. It was just the experience I needed to kneel in reverence and in silence, remembering each place and their accompanying energies, that we were honored to visit and connect to before the last and most important ceremony of all. We had made it to the end of our journey and there was only one thing left to do, the one thing we had all came for and the one thing I had been dreaming of for eight years. It was time to place the last of the seven Sacred Crystals into the Earth.

Waking up that next morning in Puno, I had so many mixed emotions. Of course, there was great excitement but also a bit of reluctance or sadness, a feeling of having carried these Crystals for so long, having spent eight years caring for them and loving them; now it was time to give the last of them to its final home. I guess I felt a bit like saying goodbye to a child who is leaving home and off to college. I didn't know I would feel this way, but I did and soon the tears were coming. I slipped outside of the hotel and held this precious Crystal in its leather covering in my arms and gave myself a quiet moment to allow the feelings of love and gratitude, as well as a bit of sadness mixed with pride to be expressed. In a way, these Crystals had been my babies, and now it was time to say goodbye. After some time had passed it was time to take a few deep breaths and clear my throat from the shakiness of my emotions and gather up the group for our trip to Lake Titicaca. It was time to take the Crystal home.

We arrived on the beautiful shores of the Lake near Puno that afternoon with the sun slowly going down and the waves crashing mildly on the beach. We found the perfect location suitable for our ceremony, where the Crystal would be undisturbed by any human activity. It was a bit of a challenge picking the exact location due to the great interest in the lake and the newly discovered underwater roadways, temples, pyramid and city. This Sacred Site in the lake is believed to be by some the lost city of Wanaku that was now attracting a lot of attention. I didn't want the Crystal to be placed in an area that would be explored or disturbed in any way and thanks to Mallku, once again, we found the perfect spot. Tucked away in a little area of the lake, we began getting ready for the ceremony. I began to think about all of the places Mallku had taken us, the different energies, technologies, sacred places and ceremonies that we got to be a part of. How precious these places and energies all were to me, to all of us, to truly have an understanding of this amazing land and peoples. Each place taught us something, or awoken something that prepared us for this ceremony.

It had been an amazing journey, and every single experience taught us something about ourselves. I looked at all the faces around me, faces that now were so familiar to me. Indeed, they were my dearest friends, my confidants, my family, hand chosen for this task from all corners of the Earth to be with me and to help me with this task and responsibility. My heart truly overflowed, to be with such good people and to be loved by them so much and to love them so fully. It was something I could never have imagined for myself while still being that little Mormon girl in 5th grade learning about a place called Peru. I took a moment just to look at them, to remember each person's energy, their face and their excitement and sense of honored duty.

Soon Mallku and I went off a bit from the group to prepare ourselves for ceremony by cleansing each other with the sage and Sacred Feathers of the Condor and Eagle. We performed our prayers and rituals, and then spoke a few meaningful words to each other before heading back to the group in the Sacred Circle. The ceremony was powerful and done by both Mallku and I as representatives of the North and the South, The Eagle and the Condor, the Mind and the Heart, coming together as one for the healing and the honoring of our beloved Mother Earth. The sacred prayers were done with all of our hearts, with all the sincerity and dedication the soul could possess. Each person in their own place started by kneeling to offer their prayers, as witnesses from the four corners of the Earth as brother and sister and as humble children of the Sacred Mother. We prayed for the healing of our Mother, for Her waters to be cleansed and respected. We prayed for the energetic leylines to be powerful and strong, for the Crystals in the Earth to carry our prayers. We prayed for humanity to move into the heart and to live as one with the natural laws and orders in the circle of life again. We prayed for all indigenous peoples, for their welfare and happiness, for them to be respected and honored, their traditions and ways to be listened to and understood by the masses.

We offered soil from different Sacred Sites from the seven continents and water from the Sacred waters from around the world, white sage and tobacco from North America as well as Palo Santo and Agua De Florida from South America. We prayed; we prayed; we prayed!

When our beloved ceremony was finished and the rituals and rites performed, my last duty as the protector and keeper of the Crystal was to seal the prayers inside with a specific offering. I took the ceremonial knife and pulled it across the palm of my hand slowly and with purpose, until the red warmth flowed easily and fell upon the Crystal. With my calling fulfilled, there was only one last thing to do, give the Sacred Crystal back to Mother. With Joyce representing the balanced feminine and my dear friend Jens representing the balanced masculine on either side of me, we walked to the water's edge. With a nod from each of them and the others praying behind us we began to walk into the lake towards an area that steeply dropped off into the deep water. With the Crystal tightly in my hands we moved deeper and deeper into the cold water. As the water rose higher and higher, I quickly spoke the last few words of an ancient prayer before the water covered my mouth and nose completely. Then.... with one last heart filled goodbye…, I opened my hands and let the Crystal slip away, to descend gently to Her new home.

Side Note:
A couple of months before our trip to Peru our dear friend Karen who was also preparing to attend lost her battle with cancer. Her last words to me were "I will be with you during the ceremony, I will be there!" As our little group walked down to the shore of Lake Titicaca on the day of the Sacred Ceremony we were surrounded by hundreds and hundreds of dragonflies. Never in my life have I seen so many, they were flying in and around the entire group. Then to my surprise, several came to land on my arms, my head and even the leather satchel carrying the Sacred Crystal. It was an impressive sight, but more than that, the dragonfly was Karen's animal totem. She was indeed with us, just as she had promised!

Part III

What Can We Do?

Time to Get to Work

No more than a couple of hours had passed since leaving the ceremonial site of Lake Titicaca before someone asked me: "So, what are you going to do now?" I was a bit taken aback by the question, knowing that the Crystals being placed in their new locations was only the beginning of what needed to be done. The truth is, now that they are in place, WE have to get to work! The Crystals were not placed into the energetic field of our planet to fix the problems of humanity. They were placed there to strengthen Mother Earth's energy and in turn strengthen humankind's energy during this incredibly important time of change. The higher Mother Earth's energy is flowing, the higher humanity is running. We are going back to the old universal truth that says: "All things are energy and the strongest energy always wins."

If we are to look back at the human consciousness and history of the last several thousand years, we can clearly see what energy has been dominant. War, greed, power, lust, pride, vengeance, the list can go on and on and on. They all have to do with one overpowering word: "Ego." Ego has ruled the human collective consciousness for a very long time. In doing so we have found ourselves in a low energy, low vibrating, inharmonious and unsustainable way of living on this beloved planet.

By placing these Crystals into the earth's leylines, embedded with our prayers of love, peace, healing, respect and honor, we not only strengthen and heighten our beautiful Mothers energetic frequency, but also heighten our own minds and bodies as well. With these crystals in place and

225

the energy on our planet getting stronger and stronger, we can clearly see the effect it has on our every thought, emotion and action. Simply put, if the earth's energy is super charged, so are you! When we concentrate our thoughts and emotions on feeding love consciousness, we will grow love consciousness! Just as the oxygen doesn't just happen to exist on our planet, it is created by the process of photosynthesis. Human consciousness doesn't just happen to exist either; it is created by each and every human action, belief, thought and feeling. We create human consciousness! When the majority of human beings act, think and place importance on ego we will live in ego consciousness. When we begin to place our attention on loving thoughts and emotions, we will grow love consciousness for all. Remember, the strongest energy always wins and now that these Sacred Crystals are activated, and in place they can support and strengthen our energy; so that we can better step into our powerful purpose and passions which will change the world for the better. The tools are now in place; the energy on our planet is growing and strengthening. Therefore we are strengthening. When we consciously choose love over hate, we will start changing the consciousness on our planet.

Yes, these Sacred Crystals have been placed into their new locations within the energetic grid systems to strengthen and heal what has been wounded, but that is not the end of what needs to be done. It is just the beginning! We need to connect ourselves more than ever to Mother Earth's energy. We need to begin our daily prayers, meditations, offerings of love and gifts of the heart. We must start focusing on connecting ourselves to the four directions, the elements and of course to our own purpose here on this planet. We can start doing so by making our own medicine wheels. Today we find our Indigenous Elders coming out of their jungles, off of their mountains, out of the great deserts and forests to teach us the importance of reconnecting to the Mother and the Sacred Sites. Far too long has humanity been ruled by ego consciousness and far too long have we harmed or neglected the very planet that sustains our lives. We must learn how to live in love consciousness once again in order to survive and thrive and be in connection with the Circle of Life. In order to do that we must go back to what is sacred.

Either we unite spiritually as a global nation, or we keep destroying our resources and with it our planet and enter a time of chaos and despair. The vision shared by our indigenous peoples is for us all to unite with one heart; for us to pray, meditate, and return to our Sacred Sites to bring forth the healing the Mother and Her children need. It is up to us to make this crucial change. The fate of the entire world depends on your decision to act! You are the Strongest of the Strong and you are essential to this world. It is important to understand both the blessing and the burden of that.

Locating Our Sacred Sites

It is time for us to locate our Sacred Sites all over this planet and start honoring them once again. I do not mean go to the pyramid and pray to the pyramid or go to a temple or a church and pray to the building because the structure itself is not sacred. No matter what Sacred Site you are at, do not look up, look down! Beneath your feet is your Sacred Mother Earth and without a doubt, each one of our ancient sites have been built in its exact location for a very specific reason: a powerful Leyline!

When we think about our ancient ancestors, and the megalithic structures and Sacred Sites that they left behind, we can see without a doubt that they had a superior knowledge to our own. Most of us think of the grand structures like the Giza Pyramids, Stonehenge or Puma Punku, but we have to start seeing the importance of *where* they are located! For decades, our fascination with pyramids and ancient structures has left us dazzled, amazed and for the most part, still confused. We are wrapped up in the mystery of it all. Who were our ancient ancestors and how did they know to build such grand structures and with such precision? Why are so many of these ancient and most significant locations built in a straight line to each other on the map? For instance, if you were to take a ruler, you could draw a perfect straight line from the Sacred Sites of Easter Island to Peru to Egypt and find that they are all aligned within one-tenth of one degree of latitude around the center of the earth. Other Sacred Sites like Mexico's Teotihuacan, the Great Pyramid of Giza and the Pyramid of Shen-Hsi in China are also aligned to each other. Not even modern technology can achieve what our ancient ancestors did so long ago. Giza alone aligns perfectly to Orion's belt and was created using the golden number, speed of light, the Fibonacci sequence and is the primary nodal point of every Sacred Site on Earth!

How astonishing is it that our ancient Sacred Sites are not only the most sophisticated human achievements, but they were also built precisely aligned with each other! Our ancient Sacred Sites share amazingly accurate building techniques using irregular blocks, some weighing hundreds of tons, which have been cut and placed perfectly together. These buildings are in alignment to the equinox, and these cultures share hieroglyphic writing, mummified bodies, astounding astrological skills and earthquake proof construction techniques, all built at a time when man had only stone hammers, copper chisels and rope. The mysteries of these places leave me with more questions than answers but also fill me with complete awe. It is very easy to say that more advanced civilizations once lived on our planet. If we were to imagine all of humanity at this time disappearing, we know that some of our buildings and structures from our modern time would last perhaps for centuries but not millennia.

The only buildings on our planet that could survive for millennia would be those whom our ancient ancestors built that we marvel at today. To this day we still do not know how these pyramids or megalithic structures were built. We only have theories in which no one seems to agree on. What we do know is that the pyramids, ancient megaliths and monuments were built on leylines, the Earth's energy grid.

The Earth contains many straight fault lines in the tectonic plates that create electric currents. These currents are called leylines or the telluric currents. We also know that the ancient structures such as pyramids, Sacred Sites and temples are all built on powerful intersecting leylines across our globe. These are our true Sacred Sites. These sites have been used for prayer, meditation, understanding and illumination of the mind and soul for thousands and thousands of years. I think we will forever be in awe of what our ancient ancestors built and wonder at the knowledge they once possessed. Underneath it all, there is the one simple truth, the reason these structures were built in these locations was because of the energy found there.

Just as our Indigenous Elders have asked us, we must go back to our Sacred Sites, not to be a tourist but to make sacred what is sacred, to say the prayers again, to connect our bodies, minds and our hearts back to the Mother. Remember, if you can not get to a Sacred Site, or you do not know where to find one, go to a hill or mountain top where the earth's energy is always very strong. Or more importantly, make one yourself! All of Mother Earth is sacred. By assembling your own sacred "Medicine Wheel" you create a place in which you can honor the four directions and elements and regain your relationship to Mother Earth. We all have the ability to create a sacred place to connect to the Great Mother, no matter where you live and no matter what your circumstances are. The place you create doesn't have to be fancy. It doesn't have to look a certain way or follow a certain tradition; the important thing is that we do it! Make your own Sacred Circle and connect.

Another great way to connect to the Mother is of course by using Crystals. We can put them in our Sacred Circles, pray with them, wear them around our necks to keep us close to the Mothers energy and help heal our wounds and illnesses. We can place our prayers and intentions within a crystal, then offer them to the water in order to distribute our prayers far and wide knowing that crystals speak to each other. As I have said before, no matter where I go on this beautiful planet I always travel with Crystals so that I can offer them to the water around the world. I have performed healing ceremonies using Crystals in countless countries, placing them in the oceans and streams, lakes and rivers in every continent. This great calling is not mine alone. We all should all be placing blessed Crystals into our water to help heal and clean that life giving, most essential element to us all. Every indigenous tribe, or group that I have met and learned from these last eight years, has shared the same desperate plea: for humankind to pray for the health and protection of our waters! For when there are no healthy waters, there are no healthy people. We must head their words and begin to pray for the waters of our beautiful planet.

Water is in everything that is alive. Within every plant, animal and person there lies that most important and imperative element, water! And within every particle of water on this planet, you can find the structure of a crystal. Those magical, transformative, powerful, life-changing crystals that can obtain, make stronger and then give out our intentions and prayers. There is a universal truth that says: "The more you know, the more you are responsible for." We all know what situation humanity is in, what situation our planet is in and why. Therefore, we are the ones responsible to fix it and we know how! So yes, it is time for us to get to work! It is up to us to take upon ourselves the individual responsibility for healing ourselves and the world we live in. It is up to us to plant that potato!

It is time for us all to lift our heads up high, with our shoulders back and believe in who we are and what our purpose in life is. We are not those who have come before us, we are the strongest of the strong. We are those who will challenge the old ways and patterns of society and strongly march forward, bringing in a new era for humanity. We did not choose to come here to sit on the bench of the biggest game of our lives. We came to make a difference, to be all that we could be. We came with passions and a purpose; we came to change the world! We can no longer be lazily blinded by TV ads that want us to be mindless consumers; we know better! We know what certain foods are making us sick and what companies benefit from our sicknesses. We know that by growing our own food or buying organic foods can keep us healthy; we know that wasting energy will only harm our planet. We know that we are beautiful just the way we are and that we do not need to give our energy to what society believes is beautiful. We know better than what has been written in our history books to be true. We know better than to follow the rules of religion that tell us what to believe and how to place one group of people above or below another. We have been born the great free thinkers of our time. We are those who have taken on the challenge of coming to this planet at this time, to correct the blind madness of the ego.

We know it within ourselves; we feel it burning from within our souls; we are the adventurers; we are the discoverers; and we are those who will not accept what someone else tells us to blindly believe. We search for truth and believe there is something better for us all. We are those who will learn to quiet the madness and to listen to the wisdom of the Elders, who will stop the consuming feelings of hate, anger, aggression and superiority and see that hate will only feed hate. We are the prophesied people who have come, the Tribe of Many Colors, who will stand as one, hand in hand with their brothers and sisters in bringing forth love consciousness back to our planet. We will not be slaves to the ways of old, but the seekers of real truth. In doing so we will bring in an era of true knowledge. It is said that: "The more loving you are the more intelligent you become." This is the foundation of why the Elders tell us that if we can move into our hearts and reconnect with the Great Mother again, we will find the most amazing discoveries; we will learn so much about where we come from and the mysteries of our world. We are the ones who have to break free from the false history we have been taught and sheeplike following of what others tell us to believe. How many generations have been taught by the Bible or the Koran or other holy books that mankind has only been on earth for 9,000 to 6,000 years? We know better than this! We know for a fact, without question that humans have been on Earth for much, much longer. So much of the information in our history books is simply untrue, but nevertheless, taught to us as fact. Modern homo sapiens occurred in Africa between 60,000 and 80,000 years ago. Evidence of man's journey out of the African continent has been documented in Australia and Central Asia at around 50,000 years and in Europe at 40,000 years! There is even substantial evidence that shows human beings inhabited North America some 50,000 years ago, long before the Clovis People, who have been thought to be the first to inhabit the continent. We have ancient artifacts like the bone flutes, animal and human figurines found in Germany that are 35,000 years old! There are also stone figures of Gia from Austria that are 25,000 years old. There are numerous others from Russia, France, Turkey, Africa and South America to name just a few that prove human beings have been here for much, much longer than what our religious books would have us believe. For goodness sake, even the city of Tiawanacu is dated to be around 17,000 years old! The ancient temple complex of Puma Punku in Bolivia was built around 14,000 years ago and constructed by using diorite. Nothing is harder than diorite, but a diamond. This ancient site was built using interlocking giant stones that were cut with laser precision and weigh up to 800 tons!

We even have human fossils dating back to 2.8 million years old and modern human footprints (not ape like footprints) found in Norfolk that are dated 800,000 years old. What about the Sumerian hieroglyphs that have been found in Peru, Puma Punku and Tiawanacu or the Ancient Egyptian hieroglyphs found in Brisbane Australia, proving our ancient ancestors were master ocean farers. Scientists have even found Egyptian mummies with cocaine and nicotine from the Americas in their stomachs. We also know that the Dogon people have known about distant planets in the solar system and the precession of the equinox since the beginning of their existence. We know for a fact that Christopher Columbus didn't discover America, nor did he discover the Earth was round. The Greeks already knew the Earth to be round for about 2000 years before Spain even existed! The list goes on and on and yet our children are being fed the same nonsense and being taught the same outdated theories, as though they were fact.

We need to begin to think for ourselves. We have to understand that we do not have to live in a box and simply believe what others tell us to mindlessly believe. Our planet's history is much richer and diverse than we have ever been taught. We are capable of so much more than what we are fooled into believing by politics, governments and religions. We must break out of the old, out of dated mold and be free to discover just how great humanity can be. We as the parents and the adults have a great responsibility to raise our children in a new way as well. The textbooks and educational exams given to our children in our school systems are designed for an "average" student when there is no such thing as an average student. Every child is different, with different skill sets and learning curves. Yet we expect them to all perform the same with one standardized education program made for the "standard" student.

We have pressured our children into "average" sized boxes far too long! We must feed their interests, value and help them thrive in their individual gifts! Our educational systems push our kids so hard in classes like calculus and chemistry when, in fact, the chances of them needing this information in their adult life are very, very slim. Why are we not teaching our children how to be healthy, happy, connected and aware, free thinking adults? Not only do WE need to connect ourselves again to the Mother and form a real relationship with the life that is all around us; Not only must WE figure out how to heal what is broken; WE must also teach our children how to do it as well! They are the geniuses, the highest vibrating souls ever to grace this planet and the change we want to see. So WE must give them the tools to be all that they can be.

So again, it's time to get to work! We are here because we are the strongest of the strong, we are the ones that must pave the way for our children to inherit a more balanced, a more loving and unified world. We must teach our children that they are unique and different and that is what makes them great, not teach them to simply conform in order to be accepted. If we want a new world for our children and a greater standard of living for them, we must create it. If our school systems will not recognize the individual greatness in our children, we certainly must! Yes, it is time for us to get to work. We can no longer simply follow along; we must lead in the way we want to live our lives and what we want to leave for our children.

The Sacred Crystals filled with our highest vibrations of love, respect, honor and our healing prayers have been put into their individual locations to help strengthen the energy grid on our planet and to help empower us. We understand the power of crystals, how they work and how we can utilize them to help heal our waters, our soils, our food and our bodies. We are beginning to understand what our ancient ancestors and our indigenous cultures have always known; we are a part of the Circle of Life; we are the elements, and we all are the children of one Mother. We as human beings are forever intertwined with our Sacred Mother. We know what is making this planet sick. We know how far humanity is pushing the boundaries of what our Mother can sustain, and we know what we are doing is wrong, so what can we do to fix it?

I find that when it comes to wanting to change our world, it is not the lack of wanting to help; it is simply not knowing what to do, that is the problem. One of the most important courses of action at this time in which we can all join in is that of healing the waters. Through prayer, meditation, unified intention and the use of crystals as well as going back to our Sacred Sites as our Elders have asked, we can start bringing about the much-needed healing. The other thing we can all do is create our own Sacred Site. By creating your own Medicine Wheel you will have a place in which you can always connect to the four elements, the four directions, to Great Spirit and to our Beloved Mother Earth. This is also a perfect place to sit quietly and connect into love consciousness. As we know, human consciousness doesn't just happen to exist, we create it! We all are creating it with every thought, every word and every emotion! What we think and say, what we give our energy to, is what will be. Therefore, it is the responsibility of us all to help create the shift from ego to a much-needed love consciousness on our planet. Once we know how it is created, we can begin taking an active part in changing it. If we all took just five minutes a day to sit down somewhere quiet and concentrated on feeling the emotions and thoughts of love, kindness, compassion and gratitude we literally could change the world. There are so many "little" things we can do to make this world a better place. This is not the time to focus on everything that is wrong with the world and wish someone would fix it. We must take an active role in what we can do to make a change in our own lives. The Elders teach us that first and foremost we must learn to BE LOVE. By being love, we feed the right consciousness on our planet. When love consciousness outweighs ego consciousness on our planet, everything will change. It is time for us to understand that our individual lives matter and that through our actions, thoughts, emotions and words, we have the power to bring forth great changes. There are many things we can do to make healthy changes in our lives and for the health of our natural world. In the next chapter I will be sharing with you my "top five" solutions to a healthier, happier, more sustainable world for us all.

The Top Five Things We Can Do to Make a Change

A: LOVE AND RESPECT NATURE!

The WWF (World Wildlife Fund) for Nature's Living Planet Index warns that the world's animal population has halved in the last 40 years as humans put unsustainable demands on the earth. Humans need 1.5 Earths to sustain our current demands. These things have already happened due to lack of natural habitat, destruction of precious eco systems, pollution, deforestation, global warming, poaching and over fishing to name just a few. If we want to stop the devastating loss of plant and animal life in the years to come we must learn to first, love the natural world and then second, protect it.

We must take an active and committed role in the health and safety of not only ourselves but also for our brothers and sisters, the flyers, the swimmers, the four legged, the crawlers, and the one legged (the trees). We are all part of a fragile balance that is very quickly becoming greatly unbalanced. We can all learn how to make a vegetable or flower garden, big or small; it does not matter. What matters is that we learn to connect ourselves once again with energy of life that abounds on this magical and Beloved Mother Earth. Simply put, the more we deeply love and value a living thing the more fiercely we will protect and honor it.

We must learn to truly love Nature again, from the smallest insect to the greatest tree! We can begin making our own sacred connection back to the Mother by creating our own Sacred Circles that represent the four directions and elements as well as visiting our ancient Sacred Sites again to help heal and magnify the powerful energies of this planet that sustain us all. You learned all about that in the first chapters of this book, now it is time to put it into practice!

B: EAT ORGANIC AND AVOID FACTORY FARMED PRODUCTS

Figures based on an analysis of government surveys show that up to 98% of our fresh food carries pesticides. This has more than doubled in the last decade! Some 46% of our fresh fruits and vegetables contain pesticide residues, up from 25% in 2003. In terms of processed food, residues were found in almost 97% of flour and 73.6% of bread! I understand that there are many of us who cannot afford to buy organic. Sadly, it is so much more expensive but if this is a possibility, it should be on the top of our list.

When it comes to consuming animal products and by-products, we should all make great efforts to only eat meat if we know the animal has had a happy life, and was not factory farmed. The meat of course is much more expensive in places like the United States and is not always as readily available in our supermarkets, but it is one of the most important things we can do! (Of course going vegetarian is the best option). If the choice is between factory farmed meat or no meat at all, I will always say NO meat!

Here are just a few reasons why staying away from

factory farm animals is SO important! The report from "One Green Planet" shows us the numerous ways factory farming is killing the environment:

Air Pollution
Almost 40% of methane emissions result from factory farming. Methane has a global warming potential 20 times higher than carbon dioxide.

Deforestation
In the United States alone, over 260 million acres of forest have been cleared to make room for crop fields, most of which are used to exclusively grow livestock feed. This is not a practice that only occurs in the U.S. Cattle ranching is now the biggest cause of deforestation in the Amazon, and nearly 80 percent of deforested areas in Brazil are now used for pasture.

Pollution
Industrial agriculture sucks up 70% of the world's fresh water supplies. Furthermore, polluted water with agricultural run-off is destroying entire ecosystems and can be toxic, if not lethal to humans and animals alike.

Animal Cruelty
The farm factories treat animals in the most cruel, horrific and inhumane ways that I have ever seen or heard of in my life. This is reason enough for me to stay clear of factory farmed meats.

C: STOP EATING SEAFOOD!

The New York Times stated in 2015: "Sea creatures sick, dying or disappearing at an alarming rate all along Pacific coast. Some wonder if it is fallout from Fukushima." The same newspaper headlines: "Ocean Life Faces Mass Extinction." And makes another statement: "We may be on a precipice of a major extinction event in marine wildlife." Back in 2006 the BBC reported: "Only 50 years left for the ocean's fish."

The ocean is the largest source of food in the world. Fish is the main source of daily protein for 1.2 billion people. However, fishermen are more and more frequently returning home with empty nets. Some scientists say that in the last 60 years stocks of large fish have fallen by 90%; they are warning that we are facing the collapse of all types of fish species in less than 50 years. The main reason for this is overfishing.

Long-line fishing vessels deploy 1.4 billion hooks a year, each with a slice of fish hanging from them as bait. There are trawling vessels that cast nets with an opening up to the size of 4 football fields. That's big enough to hold 13 jumbo jets! These nets can catch up to 500 tons of fish. Amongst the 500 tons, there is a lot of bi-catch. Bi-catch is marine creatures that are incidentally caught, often at large quantity.

Typically shrimp trawlers throw 80 to 90% of the dead marine creatures caught back over board. It is estimated that for every kilo of shrimp caught, up to 9 kilos of other marine wildlife is caught and wasted. Marine aqua-culture or fish farming is seen as a lifeline for fish. However, many of the fish that are farmed are carnivorous or eat other fish to survive. Five kilos of captured wild fish is needed to produce

1 kilo of farmed fish.

So what can we do? Very simply put, we can stop buying fish at the supermarkets, especially shrimp, shell fish and tuna! Without life in our oceans, there will not be life on land. Many people do not put the two together, but it is true. The oceans are the largest ecosystems on Earth; they are the Earth's largest life-support systems. To survive and prosper, we all need healthy oceans. Oceans generate half of the oxygen people breathe. At any given moment, more than 97% of the world's water resides in oceans. Oceans provide a sixth of the animal protein people eat. They're the most promising source of new medicines to combat cancer, pain and bacterial diseases. Living oceans absorb carbon dioxide from the atmosphere and reduce the impact of climate change. The diversity and productivity of the world's oceans should be a vital interest for humankind. Our security, our economy, our very survival, all requires healthy oceans!

D: NO MORE PLASTIC BOTTLES AND BAGS!

The Centre for Biological Diversity has stated: "Nearly every piece of plastic still exists on Earth, regardless of whether it has been recycled, broken down into microscopic bits or discarded in the ocean."

A study from the US National Library of Medicine National Institutes of Health states that a minimum of 5.25 trillion floating plastic particles weighing 268,940 tons are in the ocean. This estimate included only surface plastics, and not the materials that have sunk. An article by EcoWatch in 2016 gives us these startling facts.

- In the Los Angeles area alone, 10 metric tons of plastic fragments—like grocery bags, straws and soda bottles—are carried into the Pacific Ocean every day.
- Over the last ten years we have produced more plastic than during the whole of the last century.
- 50% of the plastic we use is used just once and then thrown away.
- Enough plastic is thrown away each year to circle the Earth four times.
- We currently recover only 5% of the plastics we produce.
- Plastic in the ocean breaks down into such small segments that pieces of plastic from a one liter bottle could end up on every mile of beach throughout the world.
- Annually approximately 500 billion plastic bags are used worldwide. More than one million bags are used every minute.
- It takes 500 to 1,000 years for plastic to degrade.
- The Great Pacific Garbage Patch is located in the North Pacific Gyre off the coast of California and is the largest ocean garbage site in the world. This floating mass of plastic is twice the size of Texas, with plastic pieces outnumbering sea life six to one.
- Plastic constitutes approximately 90% of all trash floating on the ocean's surface, with 46,000 pieces of plastic per square mile.
- One million sea birds and 100,000 marine mammals are killed annually from plastic in our oceans.
- 44% of all seabird species, 22% of cetaceans, all sea turtle species and a growing list of fish species

have been documented with plastic in or around their bodies.

- Virtually every piece of plastic that was ever made still exists in some shape or form (with the exception of the small amount that has been incinerated).
- Plastic chemicals can be absorbed by the body; 93% of Americans age six or older test positive for BPA (A plastic chemical).

So what can we do? Stop using them! There is never a reason to use a plastic sack or a plastic water bottle, not ever! The very thing that is choking our planet to death is something we humans do not even need as a necessity. You can go out and get a reusable bottle for your drinking water and bring your own cloth bags to the supermarkets. It is as simple as that. Make the decision to stop being a part of the problem and commit to it!

E: BE POSITIVE!

How many times a day, from the moment we wake up until the last thought before sleep were we negative or positive? In any situation, we can turn a negative outlook into a positive one. We have all been trained by society to think and feel the opposite. We often think: "If we just had more___ life would be better, and we would be happy." This is a lie! Many of us would see what an amazing life we have right now in this moment if we took the time to see the good. It is a mind-set that actually affects our emotions and even our health, not to mention what we attract. We think that by having "stuff" we can make ourselves happy but in truth, we are only trying to fill a void within ourselves that does not need to be there to begin with. Having more, wanting more and always looking for the next thing that will make us happy will never bring true happiness. Let us keep striving to see the positive and the good that we do have. Our culture is dead set on teaching us that by having a lot of possessions, will increase our worth. In fact, it is destroying us. For example, how often do we go to the store for one thing yet come home with several bags of stuff we didn't even know we wanted? (In a plastic bag no doubt.) Did you really need those things or did you get sucked into the consumers trap? Let us begin to share and help each other and learn to escape the: "I need more to be happy" world we have been born into. Please look over these five things and try your best in committing to one or all of them in your lives to make a greater change and impact for the good of our planet. Make a list of things you are committed to do and stick to it.

Love Your Mother, Love Yourself, Love Each Other

I have spent time in countries ravaged by war and have felt the lasting sorrow, self-degradation, mistrust, anger, sadness and poverty it leaves in its wake. I have walked the streets of oppressed nations and have witnessed the horrific treatment of children, women and animals. I have spent time with orphaned children who have been abandoned, abused and in many cases suffering from AIDS all waiting and longing for a better life. I have been to concentration camps and mass burial grounds. I have stood amongst the bleached white bones of human remains tossed into the sand like garbage by grave robbers at Sacred Sites. I have witnessed the devastating aftermath of radiation spills on not only the human population but also on flora and fauna. I have listened to Elders plead for help in keeping their sacred lands protected from logging, drug runners, pipelines, guerrilla warfare and have seen the absolute heartbreak in their eyes as they speak. I have spent time with refugees and listened to their stories of unimaginable suffering and heartbreak. I have seen and have experienced myself some of the worst humanity has to offer when ego has played its awful role. We all can think of things that are wrong with our world or the negative experiences that we have had. It is very easy to get sucked into the negative when being confronted with these things. Nevertheless, if we focus on how we can better a situation or effect change, we can focus our energy on the positive. No matter how bleak the situation is, we can choose to feed the light instead of the dark.

I am reminded of the time I visited a concentration camp in Germany. It was a very difficult thing to experience, the overwhelming sadness and fear that still lingered was almost tangible. When I thought I couldn't stay a second longer before breaking down and sobbing like a child, I decided to place a Crystal on the headstone which marked a mass grave and began to pray. No more than a few minutes had gone by when I began to hear voices talking quietly, then footsteps rumbling in the gravel next to me. I opened my eyes slightly and was overwhelmed to see people from all backgrounds, color, race, and age had begun kneeling down alongside of me to offer their own prayers. My heart and my tears could not help but overflow. Yes, there is bad in the world but there is also such great good. It is our choice to see, feel and feed the negative or the positive.

The orphanage I spent time with in Africa was filled with children who had suffered a life unlike anything we could imagine. However, there they were with giant smiles on their faces and open arms wanting a hug and a kiss. The women there were volunteers willing to teach, feed, protect and cloth each child with donated funds that came in from all over the world. The building itself was provided by a wonderful woman who refused to leave the children without a safe place to live. With her own money and through pure tenacity and determination, she had the place built and to this day watches over each child like a mother.

No matter how bad something gets, I have always been able to find those brilliant sparks of light shining brightly in a dark place. This is exactly what we have to do. Instead of focusing on the dark, let us focus on how bright our lights can shine in that dark! Yes, I have witnessed some of the worst of this world, but I have also experienced some of the best, and the best always outweighs the worst. I have had the poorest of families offer me their finest food and welcome me into their homes, as though I was an old friend. I have had refugees who have absolutely nothing, offering me their last sweets, they were able to bring all the way from Syria. I have watched people from all over the world send Crystals to Japan to help heal those suffering from radiation. I have witnessed great acts of kindness by humanity and have experienced the absolute beauty of this magnificent planet. I have been to over 40 countries, visited with countless people from all walks of life, religions and backgrounds. I've stood on some of the highest peaks of the Alps, the Rockies and the Andes. I have swam with whales and dolphins, been to numerous pyramids, temples, castles and palaces around the world. I have walked through jungles and slept in deserts. I have seen the beauty of magnificent Mother Earth in the four corners of the globe and still to this day am I left with a sense of awe and reverence in Her presence. I have learned from indigenous or aboriginal Chiefs, Mamos, Elders and Shamans from many, many different tribes all over the world who all speak with one voice in saying; we must learn to love Mother Earth and each other again.

No matter where I go or what people I meet, there is one resounding resemblance. We all are essentially good and want good things for ourselves and our families. We simply need to begin focusing our attentions on what is truly important and let the rest fall away. We need to start valuing what is important in our lives, assessing ourselves as the Great I Am, a spark and spirit that has chosen to come to this Earth to learn and grow. We must remember our own value and worth and begin to believe in ourselves once again. We need to be grateful for our bodies, our passions and purpose and use our voices to spread the seeds of those passions. Our beautiful planet is alive and flourishing because all the elements are working together to create and sustain life.

As the water freezes around the South Pole, great amounts of salty brine, rich in oxygen flow in vast cascades down to the deepest parts of the ocean floor. There this oxygen-rich salt water mixes with the lava vents which spout out tons of nutrient-rich minerals which in turn feed the smallest life forms, bacteria. Bacteria in turn feed an explosion of plankton blooms around the planet which feed the great food chain in our oceans and produce a great deal of the oxygen we breathe. Those microscopic plants which do not get eaten die off and eventually float to the bottom of the ocean floor, carrying with them all of their minerals. These precious minerals will be recycled or emerge through the hydro vents again, but some plankton will deliver their nutrients to feed our rainforests. In parts of the world like the Sahara desert where vast stretches of ancient seas have dried up, leaving only mountains of sand, we find vast remains of plankton called diatomite. Diatomite is an extremely rich source of phosphorus and as we all know, phosphorus is an element needed by all living things to produce energy. The wind lifts and carries hundreds of tons of phosphorus heavy dust high into the sky and blows it westward towards the Amazon rainforest. Each energy-rich particle of dust merges with the clouds over South America where they become water droplets. They become rain. The forest is fed and is kept healthy because of something that lived and died in the oceans.

There are so many examples of how each and every element is absolutely essential and pivotal to all life on Earth.

We can clearly see how the elements work together, stabilize and even create one another. We know that without the molten core, we would not have a magnetic field on planet Earth. We understand that the hydro thermal vents and volcanoes bring rich complex minerals, including sulfur and iron that living organisms need to survive. We know that our wind helps to create our seasons, and our storm clouds bring us rain; the winter storms bring us snow and eventually water; all that our planet needs. The wind moves our seeds, pollen and nutrients across the globe to sustain life. We know that without water, nothing could live on this beautiful blue planet of ours. We understand that the Earth itself is the container of all elements and that without Her and her bountiful gifts, we would not, COULD NOT be here.

However, how often do we realize that the elements within ourselves are just as important? You are a child of Mother Earth. You are a part of this planet, and as long as you are a human being, you too are made up of complex and interconnected elements. Your body, your Earth element, being the greatest gift Mother Earth could possibly give you, is the container of all the other elements. Your Fire element being your passion, the core of who you are, your compass in life and your flame that gives you purpose. Your Wind element being your voice, your own great spreader of seeds and nutrient that feeds and sows the seeds of who you are what you stand for and the purpose you have on this planet. Your Water element is the life-giving source, carrier and container of who it is you are. It is the crystal carrier of your words, your deeds, your beliefs and your emotions. We, just like the planet, cannot have one without the other and expect to be a healthy, creative, sustained human being. It is time for us to come home. Come home to who it is we really are and to understand this magnificent planet we know as Mother Earth.

Be happy and grateful my dear brothers and sisters. Be grateful for our world and fall in love with nature again, even if it is just by planting a flower and taking care of it. Learn to love Mother and all her creatures again. Respect the food you eat and the animals, fruits, grains and vegetables that Mother has provided for you. Treat all living things as you wish to be treated yourself, learn to love again. When there is love for all, you cannot help but want to protect and honor all. This is the way to a better life and more joy!

It is a challenge to see and feel the positive instead of the negative. I am not exempt from these things myself. I know how easy it is to think the problems of the world are too big and I am too small so what difference does it make how I live my life? We have all been there. It is important we all really try to stick to the five things we can do to make a huge impact in this world. It's easy to think: "I'm only one person and what difference can I make?" Remember, if we all would think that, nothing would ever change! We are the strongest of the strong and we can do this, let's do it together! At the end of our lives let us be proud of standing for something, for doing our best, for making a difference. Like my Great Grandma Jensen used to say: "If you do not stand for something, you will fall for anything!" Let's take this challenge together.

Try to make a commitment to some of the five things you can do and stick to it, even if it is only one out of the five, or all five. Let's do it together. Just as the African Chief once said: "Plant the potato!" Take responsibility for your own life and the impact you have on this planet. We all have a role to play and we each are affecting our planet, our human consciousness and the outcome for those who will come after us. We need to become free thinkers. We need to become aware of how precious this earth is. We need to find our purposes and passions and be able to speak our truth. We are: *The Ones We Have Been Waiting For!* We are: *The Strongest of the Strong* and we have a big mission in front of us. It is time for us to get to work! Remember your Great Mother; remember that you are not separate from Her. You are Her! You are greater than you know. You are capable and strong; you are creative and unique. You have sent yourself here to live this life with passion and purpose. You are here for a reason! It is time for us all to remember who we are and what we are capable of, because we are: *The Great I Am!* We are: *The Tribe of Many Colors*!

Love your Mother, Love yourself, Love each other and together we will change the world!

I love you,
Little Grandmother

About Little Grandmother

Little Grandmother is a world renowned spiritual teacher, a Shaman, Wisdom Keeper and the gatherer of the Tribe of Many Colors. She is the Author of the book: "Message for the Tribe of Many Colors," published in 13 different languages around the world. Little Grandmother's mission is to help re-ignite a deep remembrance in humanity of their own great potential and their personal relationships to Mother Earth. She has met with and learned from several different indigenous Chiefs, Elders, Leaders, Grandmothers and Grandfathers from all corners of the globe in order to share their messages to the people in hopes to restore and generate their remembrance of the Sacred. Her talks are freely available on the web and on YouTube and have been viewed by millions of people all over the world. You can follow her work and her many travels, ceremonies and events on her Facebook page Little Grandmother Kiesha as well as on her website: www.littlegrandmother.net. You can purchase her books at www.earthmotherpublishing.com.

(Little Grandmother does not represent any indigenous people, tribal group or individual)

Bibliography

Kottasova, Ivana. "WWF: World has lost more than half its wildlife in 40 years." CNN. September 30, 2014. Accessed February 02, 2017. http://edition.cnn.com/2014/09/30/business/wild-life-decline-wwf/index.html. Pg 239

Sean Poulter for the Daily Mail. "Up to 98% of our fresh food carries pesticides: Proportion of produce with residues doubles in a decade." Daily Mail Online. August 28, 2013. Accessed April 28, 2017. http://www.dailymail.co.uk/news/article-2405078/Up-98-fresh-food-carries-pesticides-Proportion-produce-residues-doubles-decade.html. Pg 240

Kate Good. "5 Ways Factory Farming is Killing the Environment." Http://www.onegreenplanet.org/animalsandnature/factory-farming-is-killing-the-environment. April 1, 2014. Accessed February 02, 2017. http://www.onegreenplanet.org. Pg 241

Zimmer, Carl. "Ocean Life Faces Mass Extinction, Broad Study Says." The New York Times. January 15, 2015. Accessed February 02, 2017. https://www.nytimes.com/2015/01/16/science/earth/study-raises-alarm-for-health-of-ocean-life.html. Pg 242

Black, Richard. "Science/Nature | 'Only 50 years left' for sea fish." BBC News. November 02, 2006. Accessed April 28, 2017. http://news.bbc.co.uk/2/hi/science/nature/6108414.stm. Pg 242

Marcus Ericksen. "Plastic Pollution in the World's Oceans: More than 5 Trillion Plastic Pieces Weighing over 250,000 Tons Afloat at Sea." PMC US National Library of Medicine National Institutes of Health. December 10, 2014. Accessed February 02, 2017. https://www.ncbi.nlm.nih.gov/pmc/articles/PMC4262196/. Pg 243

Nicole D'Alessandro. "22 Facts About Plastic Pollution (And 10 Things We Can Do About It)." EcoWatch. March 13, 2017. Accessed April 28, 2017. http://www.ecowatch.com/22-facts-about-plastic-pollution-and-10-things-we-can-do-about-it-1881885971.html. Pg 243

CPSIA information can be obtained
at www.ICGtesting.com
Printed in the USA
BVOW09s0103121017
497364BV00002B/129/P